To the best N
Anyone could have -
David, Johnny, Janet & John,

May EArH day bring you
closer to Jesus — And to
each other —

Kyle

Orel Hershiser, Tom Landry, John Wooden, A.C. Green,
Meadowlark Lemon, Anthony Muñoz and other famous
athletes talk about true victory and the real meaning of

WINNING

ROSEY GRIER AND KATHI MILLS

Regal Books
A Division of Gospel Light
Ventura, California, U.S.A.

Published by Regal Books
A Division of GL Publications
Ventura, CA 93006
Printed in U.S.A

Library of Congress Cataloging-in-Publication Data

Winning / [edited] by Rosey Grier and Kathi Mills.
     p.   cm.
     ISBN 0-8307-1437-5
     1. Athletes—United States—Biography. 2. Sports—Religious
aspects—Christianity. I. Grier, Rosey. II. Mills, Kathi, 1948-
GV697.A1W57 1990
796'.092'273—dc20
[B]   90-33966
                                         CIP

1 2 3 4 5 6 7 8 9 10 /X/KP/ 95 94 93 92 91 90

Rights for publishing this book in other languages are contracted by
Gospel Literature International (GLINT) foundation. GLINT also provides technical help for the adaptation, translation, and publishing of
Bible study resources and books in scores of languages worldwide. For
further information, contact GLINT, P.O. Box 488, Rosemead, California,
91770, U.S.A., or the publisher.

DEDICATION

To my children, Sheryl and Rosey, Jr.; and to my grandchildren, Keith and Kimberly—
Thanks for allowing me to be myself. I love you with a love that will never change. Always remember that who you are and what you become is up to you, but it is God's grace that gives you the choice.

—Rosey Grier

☆☆☆

To my sons—Al, Mike, Chris and Patrick—
*with *gratitude* for all the joy you've
    brought me through the years;
*with *pride* for all you have become and will
    continue to be;
*but most of all, with lots of *love*, because
    that's what you've given me.

—Kathi Mills

The publisher gratefully acknowledges the athletes, their families and the professional sports organizations who graciously provided the photographs which appear in this book. Special thanks to Rosey Grier and Kathi Mills for their tireless efforts in collecting those photos and securing permission to reproduce them here.

All photographs used with permission.

Regal Books

CONTENTS

INTRODUCTIONS:

Rosey Grier 13
"Will the Real Heroes Please Stand Up?"

Kathi Mills 17
"Jumping for Joy"

☆☆☆

Mike Barber / *Football* 23
"Reunion on the Football Field"

John Block / *Basketball* 29
"From Scapegoat to Hero"

Terry Cummings / *Basketball* 35
"A Lesson in Dependency"

Mike Davis / *Baseball* 39
"Nothing Could Be More Exciting!"

D.J. Dozier / *Baseball, Football* 45
"The Greater Miracle"

Dave Duerson / *Football* 51
"Choosing the Positive"

Keith Erickson / *Basketball, Football*   55
"A Miraculous Finish"

Vince Evans / *Football* 61
"A Boyhood Dream Come True"

Jeff Gossett / *Football, Baseball*   67
"All Things Work Together"

A.C. Green / *Basketball*   73
"One Person *Can* Make a Difference"

Rosey Grier / *Football*   79
"Free to Be Me"

Al Harris / *Football*   85
"A Powerful Decision"

Orel Hershiser / *Baseball*   91
"The Impossible Dream"

Garth Jax / *Football*   95
"No Second String"

Veronica Karaman / *Golf*   101
"Fatherly Promotion"

Joe King   107
Football, Weight-lifting, Track & Field
"Making a Choice"

Tom Landry / *Football*   113
"Something New and Wonderful"

Zeph Lee / *Football*   119
"The Right Time"

Meadowlark Lemon / *Basketball*   125
"Imitation: The Greatest Form of Flattery"

Bob Lilly / *Football*   129
"Always a Bridesmaid..."

Lamar Lundy / *Football*   137
"Finding My Source of Confidence"

"Pistol Pete" Maravich / *Basketball*   141
"A Dream Come True"

Scott McGregor / *Baseball*   147
"Counting It All Loss"

Madeline Manning Mims / *Track*   153
"Becoming a Champion"

Lenny Moore / *Football*   159
"The Best and Worst of Times"

Zeke Mowatt / *Football*   165
"Taking Advantage of My Second Chance"

Anthony Muñoz / *Football*   169
"Farther than I Ever Dreamed..."

Willie Naulls / *Basketball*   175
"To Whom Much Is Given..."

Kyle Rote, Jr / *Soccer*   179
"A Superstar Champion"

Barry Sanders / *Football*   185
"Success that Lasts"

Jay Schroeder / *Football, Baseball*   191
"A Long Shot"

Jackie Slater / *Football*   195
"Seeing Myself Through Other People's Eyes"

Jo Jo Starbuck / *Figure Skating*   199
"A Crown that Lasts Forever"

Roger Staubach / *Football*   205
"Putting It All in Perspective"

John Washington / *Football*   209
"Finding the True Source of Strength"

Reggie White / *Football*   213
"Following the Leader"

Wendy White / *Tennis*   217
"Committing My Way"

John Wooden / *Basketball*   223
"My Ultimate 'Peak' Experience"

Photo courtesy of the Los Angeles Dodgers, Inc., used with permission.

☆ **Orel Hershiser** ☆
See page 91

WILL THE REAL HEROES PLEASE STAND UP?

Introduction
by Rosey Grier

For years young people have looked to athletes as role models for their lives. In their impressionable eyes, these well-known sports figures had it all—fame, fortune, physical prowess, and success—with a capital S. But lately, all that seems to be changing. In this day of fallen heroes, admiration and confidence are quickly being replaced by disappointment and disillusionment. Kids (and even some adults) are afraid to put their trust in anything—or anyone.

And yet, there are athletes—people who, in the eyes of the world, have achieved great success—who have still managed to stand firm in their beliefs and convictions. These athletes come from different racial, economic and social backgrounds, have faced different trials and temptations, and have overcome different problems and obstacles, as they pursued their athletic careers. But each one of them, in his or her own unique way, came to the same conclusion: that there is only one way to find success, only one truth to believe in, only one life worth living. That way, that truth, and that life is Jesus Christ.

The athletes included in this book are not perfect people—they are *real people*. People who made mistakes. People who sinned. They are also people who found forgiveness for those mistakes and sins, and were then able to go on and find true victory and success and fulfillment in their lives. All of them, as they struggled to achieve success in sports, were also engaged in a struggle that is common to all mankind—the struggle to find that one missing piece in their lives that would pull all the rest of the pieces together.

I will never forget my own struggle to find that missing piece. As far back as I can remember (and these days, that's really reaching back there!), I always sensed that there was something missing. No matter how well things seemed to be going in my life, no matter how much success or fame I achieved, no matter what names I added to my list of "right connections," the feeling of permanent satisfaction wasn't there. A temporary high? Sure. Even moments of excitement and happiness. But none of it lasted. Deep down, I knew that missing piece of my life was still out there somewhere, but I just couldn't seem to find it. I also knew that, until I did, none of the other pieces would fit together and make any sense.

You see, like all the other athletes in this book, I was trying to build my life on a foundation of sand. When the real issues of life—the trials, the tests, the temptations—moved in, I discovered I had nothing solid to stand on. And so I fell. Over and over again, until finally I found the only solid foundation—Jesus Christ—and began to build my life on Him. That's when I learned that true success and satisfaction aren't based on money or fame or any of the many other changing circumstances of life, but on the One who never changes, the One who loves me no matter what I do (or don't do!), the One who never leaves me or forsakes me.

And that is the main reason I'm excited about this book. I see it as a wonderful opportunity to restore confidence to those who have been disappointed by their former role models, as well as a chance to point people in the right direction as they seek success and satisfaction in their own lives.

The other reason I'm excited about this book is that it gave me an opportunity to work with my friend and co-author, Kathi Mills (whom I teasingly refer to as the "next Pearl Buck"). Kathi has been blessed by God with an ability to touch people's hearts and lives through the written word. And through her influence in my own life, I am continuing to grow in my efforts to communicate God's love to a lost and hurting world. Both Kathi and I believe that this collection of stories from successful athletes will be an effective tool in reaching many readers with that very message— that God loves them and wants them to experience the same peace and joy and satisfaction in their own lives that these athletes have found in theirs.

Although each story in this book is different, each storyteller arrives at the same conclusion—that Jesus is the missing piece in our lives, the piece that gives purpose to the other pieces by pulling them all together into one beautiful, meaningful picture. And that's why I appreciate these athletes who took their time to contribute their stories to this book. They saw and answered the need for real heroes, heroes who are not ashamed to take a stand and declare that, without Jesus, we can never achieve true success or find permanent satisfaction. Without Jesus, we will remain incomplete, unfulfilled people, always struggling and searching for that missing piece.

And without Jesus, we will have nothing to offer our young people but a world full of broken dreams and fallen heroes.

JUMPING FOR JOY

Introduction
by Kathi Mills

All right. I admit it. I haven't always been a sports fan (or "fanatic," as my family and friends have fondly christened me). In fact, when I decided as a teenager to try out for cheerleader, it had nothing at all to do with a love for sports. I just wanted to wear one of those cute little skirts and a sweater with a letter on the front! (The jumping up and down and screaming part was a piece of cake.)

To tell you the truth, I went through my entire cheerleading career not knowing whether to yell, "First and ten, do it again" or "Hold that line." I didn't know a lay-up from a free throw, a touchback from a touchdown. And, frankly, I didn't care.

But all that changed in the summer of 1982 when my husband, Larry, came home and excitedly announced, "Guess what? I just got season tickets for the Raiders' first year at the Coliseum!"

"That's nice," I remarked, standing over the sink while I peeled potatoes for dinner. Then, without even looking up, I casually inquired, "How much did they cost?"

"Three hundred and sixty dollars," he answered.

I almost amputated my thumb.

"What?" I cried, whirling to face him. "You paid almost four hundred dollars so you could drive all the way down to L.A. and watch a bunch of guys jump on each other and fight over a stupid little ball?"

"Oh, not just for me," he went on, undoubtedly assuming that his explanation would diffuse my anger. "The tickets are for you, too." He smiled expectantly.

Obviously, we hadn't been married long enough for him to know me very well yet. But, being a trooper (not to mention the fact that I had recently read one of those how-to-have-a-successful-marriage books), I decided to give this football thing a try.

Now, there's one thing you have to understand about me. As any and all who know me will attest, I never do anything halfway. So, when we arrived at the Coliseum, I demanded a complete explanation for every play, every call, every change on the scoreboard. I studied the program until I knew the players' names and stats and positions by heart. By the end of the game, my old cheerleader training must have surfaced, because I was jumping up and down and screaming so loudly that my poor husband was beginning to get embarrassed.

But I didn't care. I was in love. I lived and breathed football. I read everything I could find about the game, the players, the coaches. I learned which teams were running teams, which were passing teams, who was being traded to whom and how those trades would affect the teams' futures. After spending all day Saturday watching college games and all day Sunday as well as Monday evening watching pro games, I would get up early the next morning and breathlessly await the arrival of the *Los Angeles Times* so I could relive the games in print.

Then it happened. My first January as a football fan. The Rose Bowl, the Orange Bowl, the Super Bowl! Could life possibly get any better?

But wait! How could this be? I came home from church the Sunday after the pro-bowl, flipped on the TV, and—there was no football! Frantically, I grabbed the paper and scanned the TV listings. Nothing!

"No more football," my husband explained. "Not until next season—the end of summer."

The end of summer! How would I survive? What would I do?

"There's always basketball," Larry suggested. "The Lakers are a great team, you know."

The Lakers. Yeah, I'd heard of them. Some big guy named Kareem something-or-other. Well, why not? I had to find some way of keeping myself from falling into a six-month depression.

Did it work? Well, suffice it to say that, a few years later when my first book was published, I skipped an autograph party because it coincided with a crucial Laker/Jazz playoff game. A couple of weeks after that, at a dinner to honor local women authors, I sat huddled in a corner chair, dressed to the teeth and trying to look inconspicuous as I held my tiny transistor radio to my ear. Even then, I managed to control myself—until the end of the game, that is, when my beloved Los Angeles Lakers defeated the Detroit Pistons in a seventh and final playoff game, making the Lakers back-to-back champions of the NBA.

I will probably never again be allowed in that

restaurant (I jumped so high, Michael "Air" Jordan would have been proud of me, and when I screamed, the busboy dropped a tray full of 18 water-filled glasses on the table in front of the guest-of-honor), but there are few times in my life that compare with the ecstasy I felt at that moment.

So, although my own physical involvement in sports is limited to four or five workouts at the gym each week, when I was offered the chance to co-compile this book with my dear friend Rosey Grier, I grabbed it. Knowing Rosey, I expected the project to be a lot of fun, but I had no idea how spiritually uplifting it would be, as well.

The testimony of each athlete included in this book has been a true source of inspiration for me. And, although their stories are all different, the message seems to be the same: the striving for excellence, the level of personal commitment that made each of these athletes great in his or her field, is reflected in a personal commitment to Jesus Christ.

This is more than a book about sports and about the people who excel in those sports. Because of the willingness of these athletes to share their testimonies, it has become a book about faith, hope and love. The Bible says that the greatest of these is love. And that love shines through in each and every story contained within these pages—love for God, for family, for friends, for country, and yes, love for sports.

But the love that flows so freely from these committed athletes is a love that puts everything into perspective—even for "fanatics" like myself. It is a love that is not afraid to stand up and declare that all the honors, all the trophies, all the accolades the world

has to offer can never compare to the joy and fulfillment that can come only from being truly loved and
forgiven, from knowing and fellowshipping with the
very God of the universe.

It's enough to make you want to jump up and
down and shout in triumph!

REUNION ON THE FOOTBALL FIELD

by Mike Barber

☆ **Mike Barber** ☆

MIKE BARBER (Football)
- All-American, All Conference—Louisiana Tech, 1974-1976
- Most receptions in single season by Oiler tight end
- Voted best tight end in Oiler history
- Played with:
  Houston Oilers 1976-1982;
  Los Angeles Rams 1982-1985
  Denver Broncos 1985
- Wife: Deanne
- Children: Brandon, Brittany

"I can't really explain it, but from the time I was seven years old, I knew I would have a career in professional sports. I had my eye on that goal even then—which just goes to show you how important eye contact is!"

THE MOST INCREDIBLE VICTORY I EVER EXPERIENCED ON a football field took place when I wasn't even in uniform. In fact, I was attending an evangelistic crusade in Houston, Texas. I had only recently become a Christian, and had been invited to give my testimony. Because it was a last-minute invitation, no one in the audience knew I was coming. But among those in the stands that night was a special young lady named Deanne—the very woman I had married in 1975, then later divorced.

Now, Deanne hadn't planned to attend that crusade, but not long before I stood up to give my personal testimony for the very first time, God spoke to her as she sat in a Bible study and impressed on her to come to the crusade. As she walked into the stadium, she heard my name announced over the loudspeaker. As I finished talking, I heard this familiar voice behind me speak my name. Before I even turned around and saw Deanne's beautiful face, I knew who it was. Shortly after that, Deanne and I were remarried.

Although I have experienced many thrilling moments on the playing field in the years that followed that time in Houston, Texas, none could ever compare to the night that God brought my wife back to me.

☆☆☆

When I was a boy growing up in White Oak, Texas, we were so poor our house leaned whichever way the wind blew. On weekends our parents sent us kids to weddings to collect rice so we'd have something to eat during the week. It didn't take much to overwhelm this country boy. Being the first draft pick of the Houston Oilers in 1976 really did it. The fancy cars, the fame, the money—it all went right to my head.

The first three years of my NFL career, I was an accident looking for a place to happen. I wasn't much for drinking, and I never got involved with drugs, but, oh, did I have a temper! If there was a fight anywhere nearby, I was in it.

I told myself I was having a great time, that I really had it all together, that I'd arrived. But way down deep inside was this longing, this loneliness, this need for something more.

Almost every evening, I'd walk into a nightclub and put on my smile and laugh real loud. But when I climbed back in my car at night to go home, I was one sad individual. I'd always thought White Oak was a real good place to be *from*, but the longer I was away from that little town and my family and all the old-fashioned values they'd taught me, the better it started to sound.

One night I was having so much trouble getting to sleep that I literally hit myself with my fist, trying to knock myself out. That's when God finally got through.

Now, I had walked the aisle of our little church back in White Oak when I was 13 years old. I made a profession of faith. I even sang in the choir. But it didn't really change my life because football was my god. But this time, as I lay sleepless in my bed at 2 o'clock in the morning, I got serious with God.

I knelt down by my bed and prayed, "God, I don't care if I never play football again. I don't care if I lose all my friends. I'm turning my life over to you once and for all."

Soon after that, my performance on the field began

to improve, which surprised me a little bit, because I'd always thought that Christians couldn't play rough contact sports. But God showed me that He wants His children to be the very best they can be, whether it's playing football or whatever. I had just as much right as anyone else to get out there on that field and play to win.

But turning my life over to Christ was the greatest victory I've ever experienced. And that's how I played throughout my career, and how I live my life today—always striving to be the very best I can be for God.

FROM SCAPEGOAT TO HERO

by John Block

☆ **John Block** ☆

JOHN BLOCK (Basketball)
- All-American—USC 1966
- Single season scoring record for PAC 8
- NBA All-Star team 1972-1973
- Played with:
  Los Angeles Lakers 1966-1967
  San Diego Rockets 1967-1971
  Milwaukee Bucks 1971-1972
  Philadelphia 76ers 1972-1973
  Kansas City-Omaha Kings 1973-1974
  New Orleans Jazz 1974
  Chicago Bulls 1974-1976
- Wife: Margie
- Children: Allison, Jeff

"My ministry now is to help young athletes move beyond a mentality that's locked into nothing more than winning and losing. I want to help them come to a point of putting their faith on the line, of recognizing the truth and importance of Colossians 3:2, which says, 'Set your minds on things above, not on earthly things.'"

LOOKING BACK ON MY CAREER IN THE NBA (WHICH IN-
cluded playing for seven different teams), I
would have to say that one of the major turning points
for me was when I was still a relatively young player
with a relatively young team, the San Diego Rockets.

Having been selected in the expansion draft by the
Rockets, I was a starter and one of the leading scorers
throughout my first three years in San Diego. As I
went into my fourth year, the team started strong.
Then, during a game, I injured my back. After missing
a few games and practices, I came back—but not 100
percent.

I was not one of those great players who could
jump back into the game after an injury and play as if
I'd never been gone. I had to "flow" back into it slowly, gaining confidence as I went along. But when the
coach finally put me into the game during the last few
minutes of the first half, I proceeded to make practically every mistake known to basketball. I stumbled,
missed the ball, let my man score, traveled—it was
horrible. We went from being six points up when I
went in to four points down at the half. I dragged myself into the locker room with the humiliating sounds
of an arena-full of "boos" echoing in my ears.

We lost 16 of the next 17 games. Every time I took
off my jersey or touched the basketball, the crowd
booed. I had become their favorite scapegoat.

Then one day I went golfing with a friend of mine,
who was also a Young Life area director. As I opened
up to him about how the fans' continual booing was
eroding my confidence and affecting my game, about
how I felt they were judging me strictly by my performance on the court rather than on who I was as a

human being, a dream was born. Out of a desire for the fans—young people, especially—to get to know the real me, I decided to start a sports camp, which would also be a Young Life camp, right there in San Diego County. Not only did that dream become a reality, it is now one of the major Young Life camps in the area.

As for my problems on the basketball court, my coach came to me one day after practice and said, "John, we've got to turn this thing around or your career is going to end." Knowing that many athletes play well against certain teams and individuals and knowing that the particular team I played well against, the Cincinnati Royals, was coming to town in a few days, I told the coach, "Don't play me tonight. Let me wait and start against Cincinnati. The fans won't boo a starter." Looking back, I know now that my response was from the Lord.

I have always admired and appreciated my coach's decision to go along with that request, because it was the turning point that brought me out of my playing slump. Not only did our team start doing better, but I went on from there to enjoy a long and successful NBA career. Following God's leading, I moved from being a scapegoat to a hero, from being stuck in depression and defeat to seeing a dream become a reality.

☆☆☆

Church and Sunday School attendance was a regular part of my life as I grew up, as was my extensive involvement in sports. I had a very supportive family, and a father who devoted a lot of time to helping me prepare for a career as a professional athlete. That's why, at the end of my last league game in my senior year in high school, my dad's sudden death was such a traumatic experience for me.

However, I realized even then what a difference my acceptance of Christ as Lord had made on the way I dealt with that loss. Only the summer before, at a Young Life camp, I had placed my faith in Jesus. Because of that, when my father died I was able to walk out onto the porch and, instead of asking why, I prayed, "Lord, help me to be strong, to help my mother and my sister through all of this."

Although I still had a lot of learning and growing to do as far as my faith was concerned, I knew at that moment—and have known ever since—that God would always be there for me, and that I could depend on Him for everything.

A LESSON IN DEPENDENCY

by Terry Cummings

☆ Terry Cummings ☆

Photo courtesy of the San Antonio Spurs; used with permission.

TERRY CUMMINGS
(Basketball)

- Forward with:
  San Diego Clippers (two years)
  Milwaukee Bucks (five years)
  San Antonio Spurs (current)
- Wife: Vonnie
- Children: T.J., Sean

*"I am who I am today, not because of anything I've done,
but because of what God has done in my life."*

MY ROOKIE YEAR WITH THE NBA WAS TURNING OUT TO be all I'd hoped for—and more. I was young, healthy, strong—and confident in my abilities. I was playing the game I loved, and I'd been nominated Rookie of the Year. Then, during a game against the Utah Jazz, I collapsed.

The doctors thought I had some sort of iron deficiency. They started me on supplements, but I still had problems. Sometimes I felt like I couldn't breathe. I was light-headed, often on the brink of unconsciousness. I was forced to miss the last seven games of the year.

That's when they put me in the hospital for what was supposed to be two hours of tests, but turned into almost five hours. As I lay there on that cold metal table, surrounded by doctors and nurses and hooked up to all sorts of machines, I realized for the first time how vulnerable I was. I didn't smoke or drink. I worked out all the time and considered myself to be in prime physical condition. But when my heart rate was mechanically elevated to 250 beats per minute and my body began to bounce up and down on the table, I suddenly knew I wasn't Superman!

I remember crying out to God, "Lord, if you want my attention, you've got it!" That's when He showed me that, no matter how strong or healthy I might have thought I was, in reality, I was totally dependent on Him. I can thank Him now for that experience because, out of it, I learned to always depend on Him.

☆☆☆

By the time I was a teenager, I had seen so much pain and hurt on the streets of Chicago that I knew it was time for me to make a decision. I was part of a gang, I carried a knife, packed a gun and fought all the time. But one night I had a dream and that dream changed my life.

In my dream, I looked up into the heavens and saw the clouds roll back. Jesus came riding out of those clouds on a beautiful white horse. He was dressed in royal apparel and carrying a scepter, and He was followed by a huge, mighty army.

As soon as I saw Him I cried out, "Lord, not now! I'm not ready!" When I woke up in that pitch-black room, I saw a tiny light over near the corner where the window was. I pulled back the curtain and looked outside. At 16 years old, with many of my friends already in jail, some even dead, I realized God was giving me a chance to do something meaningful with my life. With His help, I will continue to do just that.

NOTHING COULD BE MORE EXCITING!

by Mike Davis

☆ **Mike Davis** ☆

MIKE DAVIS (Baseball)

- Signed with Oakland A's 1977
- Outfielder with Los Angeles Dodgers (current)
- Member of 1988 World Champion Los Angeles Dodgers
- Player of the Month—April 1985
- Wife: Sandra
- Children: Nikol, Michael

"As far as the details of my sports career, it's not important for you to remember who I am, but rather, who Christ is. If you forget me, you've lost practically nothing. But if you forget Christ, you've lost it all."

I HAVE ALWAYS PARTICIPATED IN AND LOVED SPORTS, SO needless to say, I have many wonderful memories of my athletic career. But none of them compare to what I see in the future.

Based on the belief that professional athletes are in a unique position to generate the kind of resources that would enable us to actively work to help solve the many problems of our society, my good friend and former teammate Dwayne Murphy and I have started an organization called Pro-Vision. Besides providing our fellow professional athletes with numerous financial opportunities, Pro-Vision seeks to maximize the opportunity we have as professional athletes to positively impact society, and to fulfill our responsibility as role models for the disadvantaged young people of America by providing for them, not only an example, but direct assistance in breaking the cycle of poverty and impossibility that rules their lives. To be able to have a hand in shaping the future in which our children will live their lives is, for me, more exciting than anything I can imagine—even winning the World Series!

☆☆☆

My three sisters, two brothers and I grew up in a close-knit family in San Diego, California. Church attendance played no part in our lives; rather, our family life revolved around sports. On Sunday mornings, you would find my father, my brothers and me outside playing basketball in the yard. Later in the day, we moved inside to watch whatever games might be on TV that afternoon. I do remember several instances, however, where God was obviously at work in our family. But because we didn't know Him, we never gave Him the glory.

One instance in particular stands out in my mind. One of my sisters had encephalitis, an inflammation of the brain, which caused her to lose her sense of hearing and her ability to speak for a period of about four years. My parents took her to practically every doctor in San Diego. When the doctors could offer no hope, they sent her to stay with my grandmother for a summer.

Now, my grandmother was our one link to the church. She was a real "warrior in Christ," praying for all of us daily. At the end of that summer, when my sister came home, she was hearing and speaking. But, as I said, we failed to give God the glory.

Another time, one of my brothers broke his ankle so severely he had to have a screw put in it. That ankle remained swollen for about a year and a half. We had begun to think it would be like that forever. Then we went to visit my grandmother. She took one look at my brother's ankle and began to pray. Right before our eyes, the swelling went down. We were amazed, but still refused to acknowledge God's part in the healing we had witnessed.

Not only did we refuse to give God the glory when these things happened, we began to joke about it. If someone was sick or had a problem, we'd tease that we were going to tell our grandmother and have her pray. But then, one evening years later, I was forced to face up to the God my grandmother served.

It was in 1978. I had signed with the Oakland A's and was playing baseball in Modesto, California. One day I decided to drive over to Oakland and visit my grandmother. When I arrived, she was having a Bible study in her home. Since I knew no one in the area, I had nowhere else to go, so I stayed, listening to the Word of God and hearing about Jesus Christ.

When the Bible study was over, my grandmother asked me, "Mike, have you ever received Jesus Christ as your Lord and Savior?" When I told her I hadn't, she asked me if I would like to. It really didn't seem like a big deal at the time, so I agreed. Together we recited the sinner's prayer, and I asked Jesus to come into my life, to cleanse me of my sins, and to be my Lord and Savior. Then my grandmother told me to thank Him.

I said, "Thank you, Jesus."

She said, "No, really *thank* Him!"

Before I knew it, my hands were in the air and I was crying out in thanksgiving and praise to God. But Matthew 13:19 says, "When anyone hears the message about the kingdom and does not understand it, the evil one comes and snatches away what was sown in his heart." That's exactly what happened. Satan immediately began whispering things to me like, "What are you doing? If you become a Christian, you'll have to start hanging out with all those boring church people! You'll have to carry a big black Bible everywhere you go and talk all that holy-roller nonsense. You don't need that! You've got your own plan for your life. Being a Christian will only set you back."

I bought into the lie. For the next three years, although I claimed Jesus as my Savior, I did not make Him Lord. I continued to follow my own directions in life, rather than His. But in 1982 when I got involved in a Bible study, I began for the first time to really search out God's Word, trying to discover what He had to say to me personally. It hit home. I realized that my life was not in line with God's will for me, and so I rededicated my life to Him, determined to serve Him in spirit and in truth, no matter what—even if it meant giving up the game of baseball.

God has not taken me out of baseball. Instead, He has showered me with many blessings, including countless instances of His miraculous intervention in my life, both personally and career-wise. The difference is, now that I know Him, I never fail to give Him all the glory.

THE GREATER MIRACLE

by D.J. Dozier

☆ **D.J. Dozier** ☆

D.J. DOZIER (Baseball, Football)
- Parade All-American 1983 (football)
- Hertz #1 Award 1983(football)
- All-State 1982-1983 (baseball)
- All-American 1983, 1987 (football)
- Second Team All-Rookie 1987 (football)
- Running back with Minnesota Vikings (current)
- Left field, third base with New York Mets (current)
- Wife: Shelia

"It was my senior year in college before I was fully equipped—not just physically, but spiritually—to face whatever came my way."

IT WAS MY SENIOR YEAR AT PENN STATE AND WE WERE IN South Bend, Indiana, ready to take on Notre Dame. Due to a knee injury, I wasn't expected to play. God, however, had other plans. He miraculously healed my knee, enabling me to go on and play the game. But as wonderful as that miracle was, an even greater miracle had taken place just the night before.

I was a fairly new Christian, as was my roommate, Tim. We hadn't really spent any time trying to witness to our friend and teammate Greg about the Lord, but that evening, Greg came to see me.

"D.J.," he said, "I need to talk to you."

We went to his room and he began to tell me some of the things he had done in his life, things he felt terrible about. He wanted to know what to do. When I explained to him about asking God to forgive him, Greg began to weep and to pour out his heart to God. Once again, he asked me what to do.

"Give your heart and life to the Lord," I told him. He agreed.

I called Tim, and the three of us went down to the chapel where we prayed together and Greg committed his life to Jesus Christ. Since that night, the three of us have grown tremendously in our relationship with the Lord, as well as with each other—as friends, as brothers, and as men of God.

☆☆☆

Although I first accepted the Lord and was baptized at the age of 10, I never spent any time learning about Jesus, so over the years I drifted further and further away. By the time I left high school and went on to college, football had become the most important thing in my life, the closest thing I had to a god.

By my junior year, however, I had begun to sense that there was something missing in my life, but I had no idea what it was. Then one night I walked into my room and saw my roommate, Tim, reading a Bible. Suddenly, I knew what was missing—it was God. So I began to read my Bible, to pray daily and to attend church regularly. Still, I sensed that things weren't quite what they should be.

In spite of that, when our football team went on to the National Championship against Oklahoma and one of my teammates scored the first touchdown, I knelt down in the end zone to give thanks. When I got back home after the game, I went to the Sunday night service—although I made it a point to sit way in the back, in the very last row in the balcony.

Toward the end of the service, I began to pray. "Lord," I complained, "why have I had so many injuries during my career? Why haven't you protected me so I could go out on the field and be my best? Why would you give me this talent and then not allow me to show people what you've done for me so that I can give the glory to you?" The more I prayed, the angrier I became. And then the pastor, who had also been praying, looked up and called out my name.

"D.J., are you here?" he asked.

From the very back of the church, I waved.

"D.J.," he went on, "the Lord has just spoken to me about you. He told me to tell you that if you were as bold for Him as you are in the sport you play, He would give you all you need. If you will put Him first in your life, He will exalt you above measure."

That's when it all fell into place. I realized that God wanted more from me than lip-service—more than daily Bible reading and prayer and church attendance—what He wanted was my heart. All of it. And so I gave it to Him, then and there.

It wasn't long after that I found myself in another championship game—the game in which we won the '86-'87 National Championship. When I scored the winning touchdown, I knelt once again in the end zone. There on my knees, as I gave thanks and glory to God, He used that moment in a way I would never have dreamed. Pictures of me in that kneeling position before my Lord became a mark in Penn State history. One company took the picture and made posters of it, sending it throughout all of Pennsylvania to businesses and stores everywhere. God had kept his Word and allowed me to be exalted in a way that gave all the glory and honor to Him—and that's as it should be.

CHOOSING THE POSITIVE
by Dave Duerson

☆ **Dave Duerson** ☆

DAVE DUERSON (Football)

- Captain, MVP—Fighting Irish 1982
- All-American 1981-1982
- All-Pro 1985-1988
- NFL Man of the Year 1987
- NFL Players Association Humanitarian of the Year 1988
- Wife: Alicia
- Children: Chase, Tregg, Brock

*"My career is not my own. It is a gift
to be shared with others."*

AS MUCH AS I HAVE ENJOYED MY FOOTBALL CAREER, I'VE always tried to think of my athletic success as a foundation on which to build or set an example for others. That's why, when I'd lost four of my friends through drug-related incidents, I decided it was time to do something constructive, something to offset the negative. And so, along with my father, Arthur, and my brother, Michael, we formed a non-profit organization known as DAMCO (for David, Arthur and Michael).

To me, DAMCO is one of the most important aspects of my entire career. Although DAMCO is set up primarily to offer free football camps for kids, the emphasis is on the necessity for building a drug-free society and the importance of a good education.

You see, professional athletes are in a position to influence a lot of lives—young lives, especially. That influence can be positive or negative, and can be passed on both verbally or by example. I believe that those of us who have been blessed with this sort of athletic success have a responsibility to live lives that encourage and inspire those who are watching us to strive to become all that they've been created to be.

☆☆☆

Although I first accepted the Lord when I was eight years old, I didn't truly come to understand the magnitude of God or the importance of having an ongoing relationship with Him until many years later, when I was an undergraduate student at Notre Dame.

So many of the courses I was studying—particularly in philosophy—encouraged me to question the existence of everything, including God and, ultimately, myself. But thanks to the influence of some Christian friends, including Coach Dan Devine, I eventually locked myself away in a motel room and began to search through the Gideon Bible for the answers I needed.

As I opened and reopened the Bible at random, Scripture after Scripture spoke to my heart as surely as if God Himself were standing in that room next to me, whispering in my ear. One verse in particular, Psalm 23:4, seemed to jump right out at me:

> *Yea, though I walk through the valley of the*
> *shadow of death, I will fear no evil: for thou*
> *art with me; thy rod and thy staff, they*
> *comfort me (KJV).*

Suddenly I realized that, not only did I truly exist, but I existed as a very special person because the very God of the universe had created me and died for me—for *my* sins! My God-knowledge was no longer generalized knowledge. It was personal knowledge, because it had come down to just Him and me—and that's about as personal as it can get.

A MIRACULOUS FINISH

by Keith Erickson

KEITH ERICKSON
(Basketball, Volleyball)

- Honorable Mention, All-American
  UCLA 1965
- Played with:
  UCLA 1963-1965
  U.S. Olympic Volleyball 1964
  San Francisco Warriors 1965-1966
  Chicago Bulls 1966-1968
  Los Angeles Lakers 1968-1969,
    1972-1973
  Phoenix Suns 1973-1974, 1976-
    1977
- Wife: Adrienne
- Children: Sean, Angelica, Forest,
  Gloria, David

"The world is crumbling around us because people can't find a solid foundation on which to build their lives. Instead, they're turning to drugs, adultery, suicide— anything to ease the pain. That's why it's up to us to live lives that will point them in the right direction."

WHEN YOUR ATHLETIC CAREER INCLUDES PLAYING under the greatest coach to ever oversee a basketball team—John Wooden of UCLA—plus 12 years in the NBA with such teams as the San Francisco Warriors, the Chicago Bulls, the Los Angeles Lakers and the Phoenix Suns, you are bound to possess an abundance of outstanding memories. I think the one that means the most to me, however, was when I was in a playoff game with the Phoenix Suns against the defending NBA champions, the Golden State Warriors in 1976.

No one had expected us even to reach the playoffs, let alone give a team like the Warriors any real competition. But I had prayed for a chance to give God glory through my efforts that day, and there we were, down to the last few seconds of our most critical playoff game. We were only down by two points and we had possession of the ball. It was our big chance.

I was standing directly under the basket when the ball was passed straight to me—right through my hands and out of bounds. *That was it*, I told myself. *It's over now.*

But as soon as the other team took possession of the ball, we fouled immediately and sent one of their guys to the free-throw line. He missed. We were still alive.

With about five seconds to go and no time-outs left, the ball was inbounded and thrown down-court to me. I was standing right in front of the Golden State bench and I could hear the coach yelling, "Don't foul him!" My reputation was not that of a shooter—I was more of a defensive player—so the smart play was to let me shoot and absolutely not foul me where I'd have a chance at two free throws.

As time ran down, I let the ball fly and just as the

buzzer sounded—*Swish!* The game was tied up and we went into overtime.

Time and again throughout the overtime period, the ball came to me. And time and again, I scored. The cry from the Golden State bench had changed from "Don't foul him!" to "Get on him!" and "Don't let him shoot!"

No one was more surprised at my newfound marksmanship during that overtime period than I was. When the newspapers announced our victory the next morning, the headlines referred to the game as being nothing short of "miraculous." As far as I'm concerned, that's exactly right. It was God's victory, and I give Him all the glory.

☆☆☆

Born and raised in Southern California, I grew up in a "good" family—close-knit, morally respectable—we even went to church two or three times a year. It was a good life, and my childhood was a pleasant one.

I became involved in sports early-on, including tennis, volleyball, baseball and basketball. I spent every free minute at the beach. In fact, I spent as much time "playing" as I could, and as little time studying as possible. So, when high school graduation rolled around, I didn't receive any scholarships. Instead, I spent a year at junior college before receiving my one and only scholarship offer to UCLA, where I was privileged to play on their first two NCAA championship basketball teams.

But it wasn't until I had begun my 12-year career in the pros that I began to look around and wonder if there was more to life than the material success I was beginning to experience. Having had a roommate at one time who professed to be a Christian but lived no differently than any of the rest of us (with the exception of attending church on Sunday mornings), I decided the answers to life were not to be found in Christianity.I then turned to cults, the occult and witchcraft, none of which provided me with the answers I was looking for, either. In 1973 I was traded from the Lakers to the Suns. About that same time, I met a nutritionist at my basketball camp. He had a gym, and I began working out with him on a regular basis. I also began asking him a lot of questions. One day he pulled his Bible out from under his desk and began to share with me from the Word of God. The more I heard, the more excited I became.

It was the first time I had thought of my life in relationship to God. It was the first time I had really heard the message of Jesus Christ—of why He came to earth, lived a sinless life, then died and rose again. It was the first time I realized He had done all those things for me, that I might have my sins forgiven and have His righteousness within me.

It was the beginning of a new life for me and for my family. And it answered the questions that had nagged at me for so long—answers that I could not find in the world no matter how hard I searched, because Jesus was the only answer I needed.

A BOYHOOD DREAM COME TRUE

by Vince Evans

☆ **Vince Evans** ☆

VINCE EVANS (Football)

- Hall of Fame Award, L.A. City College 1973
- MVP Award, Rose Bowl, Sr. year at USC
- Athlete of the Year 1981 (while with Chicago Bears)
- Inspiration to Youth Award 1988
- Played with:
    Chicago Bears (seven years)
    Los Angeles Raiders (three and-a-half years)
- Wife: Chyla
- Children: Chloe, Vincent Jordan

"Of all the things that have ever happened to me in my lifetime, the most awesome was the realization that the very God who created the heavens and the earth loved me so much that He wanted to come and live inside of me."

A S FAR BACK AS I CAN REMEMBER, THROUGHOUT MY growing-up years in Greensborough, North Carolina, my favorite place to be was right in front of the TV, watching college football on Saturdays and pro games on Sundays. But the game that stands out most vividly in my mind was a play-off game between USC and UCLA. The winner would secure a berth in the Rose Bowl.

As usual, I was positioned in front of the TV set, caught up in the excitement of the game. UCLA was ahead, with only minutes to go, when the USC quarterback handed off to their star running back, O.J. Simpson. Racing down the field for a 64-yard touchdown-run, O.J. sewed up the win for USC. As the crowd roared and the beautiful white Trojan horse galloped around the field in triumph, I nearly burst with youthful exuberance. "Dad," I announced suddenly, "I'm going to play football for that school someday!"

My father just looked at me for a couple of minutes and then replied, "You're nuts."

But the dream had been born, and years later as a junior at USC, I had my first real opportunity to play for the school I had dreamed of attending. As the season progressed, however, our team went to 8 and 4, and the dream turned to a nightmare. Although 8 and 4 might not have been bad for some colleges, USC was used to winning. A record of 8 and 4 was unacceptable. I began to receive hate mail, and everywhere I looked I saw bumper stickers that read, "Save USC football—Shoot Vince Evans."

It was scary, but I wasn't about to give up my dream that easily. I came back the next year and led the team to a victory at the Rose Bowl, where I was awarded MVP of the game. My boyhood dream had finally come true. But deep down, I sensed that something was still missing....

☆☆☆

From USC I was drafted by the Chicago Bears. My dream seemed to be getting bigger and better all the time. In fact, I was sure I had "arrived." After all, I now had enough money and success to be able to live in the best neighborhoods, drive expensive cars, wear classy clothes, hang out with the "right" people—my ego was so inflated I had become my own god! Then, in 1979, things began to change.

We were down in Miami playing the Dolphins. During the game I received a deep cut on my arm, but other than applying some antiseptic, I didn't pay much attention to it. Back home that night, however, I woke up in the early morning hours in so much pain I literally had to crawl to the bathroom. When I was finally able to call some friends to take me to the hospital, I was diagnosed as having a staph infection. My temperature soared to between 105 and 106 degrees. Conceivably, the infection could have gone to my brain or heart. Instead, it settled in my back, and I was treated with antibiotics.

Never having been in a hospital before, it was a humbling experience to find myself so weak that, after a one-month stay, I had to depend on a walker to get around. Suddenly, the god of "self" that had always served me so successfully was no longer sufficient to meet my needs. I went home from the hospital on Easter Sunday, still asking myself the question, "Why? Why me?"

And then I turned on the TV, only to hear a preacher speaking about the resurrection of Christ. Although

I had been raised in a Christian home and had a praying mother who interceded for me daily, I had never made a personal commitment to Jesus Christ. But as I heard that preacher say, "Jesus Christ died for your sins," I began to weep like a baby. I remembered what I'd heard people say about the "God-shaped vacuum" within each of us, and I realized what had been missing all those years. I'd been trying to fill that vacuum with everything else, and it hadn't worked. Now, as I asked Jesus Christ to come into my heart and to fill me with Himself, I felt a huge weight lift from my shoulders. For the first time, I was truly free. No longer did I have to prove anything to anybody, because with Jesus dwelling inside me, I was complete. The God-shaped vacuum had been filled.

ALL THINGS WORK TOGETHER

by Jeff Gossett

☆ **Jeff Gossett** ☆

Photo courtesy of the Los Angeles Raiders; used with permission.

JEFF GOSSETT
(Football, Baseball)

- All-American 1978 (baseball)
- Led nation in Punting Division II 1977
- Drafted by New York Mets 1978
- Played football with:
  Kansas City Chiefs 1981-1982
  Cleveland Browns 1983, 1985-1987
  USFL 1984
  Houston Oilers 1987
  Los Angeles Raiders (current)
- Wife: Jeanne
- Children: Alexis, Natalie

"If there's one thing I try to stress over and over again to kids, it's that you will become like the people you hang out with."

WHEN I TRIED OUT FOR MY FIRST NFL SPOT IN 1980 with the Dallas Cowboys, I was a brand new Christian. Being cut from the team after only four pre-season games was a devastating experience. Why? I asked the Lord, over and over again. Why is this happening to me? And then, in 1981, the same thing happened again. After signing with the San Diego Chargers as a free agent, I was let go after four pre-season games.

This time I began to seek my answers in the Scriptures. In the meantime, I was signed by the Kansas City Chiefs, where two very strong teammates helped me grow in the Lord.

Since playing with the Chiefs, I have also played for the Cleveland Browns, the Houston Oilers, and now the Los Angeles Raiders. Looking back, I can see the wisdom of God's timing. Each step of the way, He led me to the right place at the right time, where I was able to fellowship with committed Christians, like the great group we have on the Raiders right now.

I don't have to ask why anymore. The truth of Romans 8:28, "And we know that all things work together for good to those who love God, to those who are the called according to His purpose" (*NKJV*) has become evidently clear to me.

☆☆☆

Before joining the NFL, I played for two years at the minor league level with the New York Mets. It was there that I began attending Bible studies with some of the guys on the team, listening and learning about God. But it wasn't until the Mets forced me into a decision about my career that I finally made another decision—a decision that would ultimately affect me for all eternity.

I was playing third base when I was approached by the Mets to switch over and play pitcher. I didn't want to do that, so I quit baseball altogether, climbed into my car, and started the long, lonely drive back to Illinois from Florida.

I couldn't believe it! I was walking away from all I had worked for my entire life. Worse yet, I had no idea where I was headed. Somewhere between Florida and Illinois, I turned to God.

"I'm lost," I told Him. "I don't know what to do, which way to go. Please come into my life now and take over from here on out. I'll follow you wherever you lead me."

Never once has He left me or let me down. Never once has He steered me in the wrong direction. Never once have I regretted my decision to follow Him.

Photo used with permission.

☆ **Meadowlark Lemon** ☆
See page 125

ONE PERSON CAN MAKE A DIFFERENCE

by A.C. Green

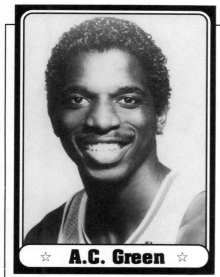

☆ **A.C. Green** ☆

Photo courtesy of the Los Angeles Lakers; used with permission.

A.C. GREEN (Basketball)

- Pac-10 Player of the year, junior year, Oregon State
- Voted third team All-American by AP and UPI, senior year, Oregon State
- Region 8 Player of the Year
- NBA All-Defense second team, 1988
- NBA All-Star team 1989/90 season
- Starting forward with Los Angeles Lakers

"I'm looking forward to the day when athletes are admired, not so much for their talents and abilities, but for their moral structure, their integrity and their character."

PLAYING FOR THE LOS ANGELES LAKERS, THERE ARE A lot of games that stand out in my mind, but one of the clearest memories I have is of a game we were playing against one of our Pacific Division rivals. We were down by about 15 points at half-time, and it seemed like we just couldn't do anything right. Instead of sinking free throws, we bounced the ball off the backboard. Our passes were being intercepted by the opposing team and returned for easy buckets. Neither the coaches nor the players could figure out what we were doing wrong.

And then, suddenly, I remembered what I had been talking to my teammates and coaches about for the last year or so. I'd been telling them how one Man—Jesus—had made such a difference in so many lives. The reason, I told them, was because He had a mission, and that was to obey God's call on His life.

The more I thought about it, the more sure I was that God was calling me to take a step of faith, to prove that I believed what I'd been telling everyone else—that one person really can make a difference. With Jesus Christ as my example, I decided to act on my faith.

The minute I made that decision, I felt new life flowing through me. I was excited! I started slapping "high-fives" with everybody and telling them we were going to win the game. They just looked at me like they thought I'd been drinking too much Gatorade or something. But as we began to close the gap on our opponents, with only six minutes to go in the game, I could tell that my teammates were beginning to believe what I was telling them—we really could win that game! Even the coaches were so excited they began slapping high-fives! Everyone was yelling, "We can do it! We're going to win!"

And we did. With only 30 seconds to go, we went ahead by one point. The rest is history.

I've never forgotten what I learned that night, and I never will. On or off the court, the way I choose to live my life has a tremendous effect on those who are watching me. You see, I'm not in a position to choose whether or not I want to be a role model. It goes with the territory. The only thing I can choose is what type of role model I want to be, and what kind of difference I want my life to make for others.

☆☆☆

I wish I could say that going to church had always been a priority in my life, but that's just not so. Although my parents insisted that my two older brothers, my sister and I attend church every Sunday, I tried every excuse in the book to get out of going—stomach aches, staying up late on Saturday nights to watch scary movies on TV, sleeping over at a friend's house—but nothing worked. And so, we went— "faithfully."

Until I started high school, that is. Then my parents left it up to me to decide. And guess what? I decided that I just didn't need to go to church. I was much more interested in playing sports and hanging out with my friends. I had more important things to do.

By the time I graduated from high school, I had several scholarship offers to various colleges, mostly on the West Coast, which is where I wanted to stay. I chose Oregon State. But that summer—1981—before leaving for college, I took a short trip with some friends to visit a former teacher and football coach, Rod Brogado, in a little town called Hermiston, Oregon.

The first thing Rod told us when we arrived was that we were going to have a lot of fun that weekend, but we were also going to have Bible studies. That was all right, but on Sunday morning he informed us we were all going to church. I argued that I couldn't because all I had brought with me to wear were shorts. Rod, who stands about 5'7" and weighs about 180 pounds, insisted I could wear some of his clothes. Since I was 6'8" and weighed around 215 pounds, I decided he must be pretty determined for me to go to church if he was willing to make an offer like that! So I went—in my own shorts, of course.

The sermon was titled "Do You Want to Go to Heaven or Do You Want to Go to Hell?" Looking back, I know that no other sermon could have had such a heavy effect on me as that one. It was exactly what I needed to hear, because up until that day I assumed that you got into heaven if you were basically a good person—you know, if you didn't fight too much or drink too much or raise too much havoc, commit too much immorality. Compared to most of my friends, I was an angel!

But suddenly I realized that it wasn't what I did or didn't do in comparison to other people. It was what I did with the truth of Jesus Christ. As I listened to that pastor, I felt challenged in my soul to leave compromise behind, to quit being led by friends and influenced by peer pressure, to stop worrying about what people would say or what they would think of me.

As the pastor gave the altar call, asking people to come forward and make Jesus the Lord of their lives, I wanted to go. I took one step, then stopped, still afraid that my friends would laugh at me. The pastor gave another altar call. I tried to move, but I could hear the devil whispering to me, "Let someone else go first." A third altar call, and then a fourth. Finally, I stepped out into the aisle and began to make my way to the front—which wasn't very far, since I had been sitting in the second row! But, even today, I remember it as being the longest walk of my life.

As long as that walk seemed, though, it is one I have never regretted. For the first time, I had come to know and experience Jesus Christ. And I had made a commitment to do what was right and to honor God in all that I would do from that day on—no matter what.

FREE TO BE ME
by Rosey Grier

☆ **Rosey Grier** ☆

Photo used with permission.

ROSEY GRIER (Football)
- All-American, high school 1951
- All-American, Penn State University
- All-Pro (four times)
- Played in five World Championship games
- Athlete of the Year 1962 (while with N.Y. Giants)
- Elected to New Jersey Sports Hall of Fame 1971
- Meritorious Service Award 1978
- Member of most honored line in pro football: "Fearsome Foursome," Los Angeles Rams
- Wife: Margie
- Children: Sheryl, Rosey, Jr.

"We all have an opportunity, because of the power of God inside us, to make this world a better place. Each life that we touch makes a difference."

I'VE PLAYED NUMEROUS COLLEGE AND PROFESSIONAL football games throughout my career, but one game stands out in my memory for a very special reason. It was a game in which my dream and the dream of every defensive football player came true.

As a defensive specialist and a member of the Los Angeles Rams' "Fearsome Foursome," I was facing the Green Bay Packers in the Coliseum, hoping to break an eight-game losing streak. Near the end of the game, the Packers pushed us down to our five-yard line. Bart Starr was at quarterback, and, since Bart had a way of throwing touchdown passes, we figured it was time for a blitz, a play where everybody rushes into the backfield and jumps on the quarterback. So Bart came out of the huddle and yelled, "Hut! 2-8-4, 2-8-4. Everybody go down." And his offensive line got down into position for the play they had just plotted in the huddle.

He took the ball and yelled, "Hut two, hut two!"

Then he backed up with the ball and closed his eyes. While he had his eyes closed, probably thinking, "I'm going to throw a touchdown over the Fearsome Foursome," he heard a voice speak to him.

The voice said, "You'd better open your eyes."

He opened his eyes and, staring in his face, was Deacon Jones. Now Deacon Jones didn't have anything against Bart personally, but he was generally furious with all quarterbacks. So he leapt on Bart. Then Merlin Olsen leapt on him. And finally, for good measure, Lamar Lundy leapt on him. That left nowhere for me to leap on him. And, just as I was about to feel sorry for myself (almost as sorry as I imagine Bart was feeling for himself at that moment), the ball popped up in the air.

I thought, "Wow, there's the ball and all my life I've been wanting to carry the ball. I'm going to get that ball and go down that sideline, and I'm going to say, 'Hey, Mama, what's happening?'"

Now, there is no shout louder, no cheer more joyous, no applause more glorious than for the man who carries the ball for a touchdown or a significant gain. And so, we whose specialty it was to ruin the best efforts of these gallant and fleet-footed men always hungered and thirsted for the rare opportunity to grab that ball and do with it what they did.

The ball struck my hand and fell to the ground. The referee's whistle was still silent—it was a live ball. I jumped on it and covered it up. There it was again, in my arms!

Then I heard a voice say, "You can still make it."

I jumped to my feet and started to make my getaway.

A second voice spoke. "Better see who's coming after you."

I looked around and got my answer. All 11 of the Green Bay Packers were coming straight for me. I was in imminent danger of getting a taste of my own medicine!

Suddenly I wanted nothing better than to be rid of that accursed ball. Seeing no one to whom to toss it, however, and being too proud to fall on it a second time or to throw it out of bounds, I ran for my life. Then, THUD! The first Packer to reach me hit me with a force I'd never felt before. In a moment, they were all on me with merciless ferocity—seeking to avenge the loss of the ball before they had to leave the field and give place to their own defensive squad. Their vengeance must have been sweet because, when they finally pulled everybody off of me, blood was pouring from my mouth. I had bitten clean through my own tongue!

But something good came of that incident—besides the fact that the Rams recovered and regained the offensive and, eventually, went on to win the game. The good I have in mind was more personal and internal. It consisted in my being entirely set free from coveting the work of the ball carrier. I was, at last, content to be a defensive tackle.

Becoming free to be who I am is a lesson I have incorporated into my personal life many times since.

☆☆☆

It was in 1978, after having divorced my second wife, Margie, that a friend brought me a Bible and told me to read it. I didn't pay much attention to him, but when an airline stewardess I didn't even know came up to me during a flight and told me the same thing, I began to wonder. When she asked me for my phone number, I gave it to her, not really expecting to hear from her again.

One Sunday morning soon after that, however, my phone rang. It was the husband of the airline stewardess. He said his wife had asked him to call and tell me to watch a program on television. I'm not sure why, but I agreed.

I turned it on and heard Dr. Frederick K.C. Price talking about a particular verse in the Bible—John 3:16. I picked up the Bible my friend had left with me a few weeks earlier and looked up the Scripture. It spoke of God's promise of everlasting life.

It wasn't long before my son, Little Rosey, began watching the program with me every Sunday morning. Soon, he convinced me to visit Dr. Price's church; before the service was over, both Little Rosey and I had given our hearts and lives to Jesus Christ. Soon after that, Margie came to church with us. She, too, made a commitment to Christ, and, on June 8, 1981, we were remarried.

Thanks to the love and grace of God, our family was reunited once again.

*Adapted from *Rosey: The Gentle Giant* by Rosey Grier (Tulsa: Oklahoma: Harrison House, 1986). Used by permission.

A POWERFUL DECISION

by Al Harris

☆ **Al Harris** ☆

AL HARRIS (Football)

- All-American, Arizona State 1978
- MVP, Arizona State 1978
- Unsung Player of the Year 1988 (Chicago Bears)
- Played with:
  Chicago Bears 1979-1984, 1986-1988
  Philadelphia Eagles (current)

"It's easy to find ourselves doing something we know is wrong, but still not be willing to give it up, because there's nothing to fill the void that's left behind. But when someone offers us love to fill that void, how can we turn it down? Love is a great motivator."

I WAS A FRESHMAN IN HIGH SCHOOL—MY FIRST YEAR OF really playing football. Before that, my sports activities consisted of sporadic games of "street ball." You know, the kind where you can quit and go home whenever you want to. But organized sports is different. I hadn't yet learned that, when you commit to play on a team, you can't just quit and go home when the going gets tough.

It had been a year of change for me. The summer before my freshman year, I grew from 5'10" to 6'3", even though I hadn't really filled out yet. And my shoe size went from a 10 to a 13. I looked like a clumsy, overgrown pup whose body hadn't caught up with its huge paws! Because of my size, the coach decided I was too big to be a running back or a receiver, so he switched me to offensive guard. I wasn't used to the position, and I ran the wrong way, colliding with another guard. The coach was furious. He screamed at me and kicked me off the field.

That's it, I thought. *I quit!* And I went home to tell my mom of my decision.

Being a typical mother (and not too crazy about the idea of my playing football, anyway), she was understanding and sympathetic. My dad's response, however, hit me right between the eyes.

"If it's too tough for you, Son," he said casually, "if you can't take it, go ahead and quit."

If it's too tough for you... If you can't take it... The words rang in my ears, echoing through my mind over and over again.

I will not let them make me quit! I decided. *I will not let them drive me off that field! If I ever quit football, it will be because I want to, not because someone else forced me to!*

It was the first time I had ever made a decision with

power behind it. It was the first time I had ever really made a commitment of that magnitude—and followed through. As I learned to live and move within that commitment, I discovered talents and gifts I didn't even know I possessed. Because my attitude had changed, I soon found myself honored as one of the stars of the team.

Even more important, when I became a Christian years later, I was able to apply what I'd learned on the football field to my spiritual life, as well. As I committed myself to walk in God's paths, I discovered talents and gifts I didn't know I possessed, and God was able to use me in ways I'd never before imagined.

It was the most powerful decision I ever made.

☆☆☆

The first time I truly recognized that there was a God was not long before I graduated from high school. I was living in Hawaii, one of the most beautiful places in the world. I stepped outside one night and looked up into the heavens. The stars seemed close enough to touch. I thought about creation—the sun, the moon, the planets, the ocean, animals, humans, the seasons—and *I knew* it was no accident. But when I began to think about death, about where I would go when my life on earth was over, I turned away. I was not yet ready to deal with anything so heavy.

Throughout the next few years, God brought many people into my life to draw me to Himself. While attending Arizona State University, a lovely young woman came up and invited me to attend a Bible study. I wasn't really interested in the Bible study, but I was interested in her, so I went. Although I didn't accept the Lord right away, I was impressed with the people I met. Instead of spending their time talking about themselves, they were excitedly talking about God, as if they truly knew and loved Him.

Many others, including Greg Ball from Maranatha Ministries and fellow teammate Vince Evans, told me time and again of God's great love for me. They never came up and said, "You shouldn't be doing this or that," they just said, "God loves you so much that He sent His very own Son to die for you."

Finally, one night in August 1981, I prayed, "God, I don't know much about you, but I know I'm a sinner and I believe Jesus died for my sins and was raised up so I could have eternal life. I want to know you, God. I ask Jesus into my heart now."

It wasn't until sometime later that I found out about how my Christian grandmother had read Scriptures to me over and over again at a time when many people would have thought I was too young to retain anything she said. But the seed of the Word was planted. Throughout the years, many people came along and watered that seed. And in God's time, that seed sprouted and brought forth fruit.

The Bible says that there is a season for everything. As I look back to that night in Hawaii when, through His creation, I first became aware of the reality of God, I know my season has come.

THE IMPOSSIBLE DREAM

by Orel Hershiser

OREL HERSHISER (Baseball)

- Cy Young Award 1988
- MVP, playoffs and World Series 1988
- *Sports Illustrated's* Sportsman of the Year 1988
- *The Sporting News'* Major League Player of the Year 1988
- Associated Press Male Athlete of the Year 1988
- Pitcher with Los Angeles Dodgers (current)
- Wife: Jamie
- Children: Orel Leonard V "Quinton," Jordan

"I have to deal with reality and the fact that I'm only human, just like any other athlete. But still I push to be the best Orel Hershiser I can be, and I never want to settle for less."

WE WEREN'T THE BEST TEAM IN THE MAJOR LEAGUES. We were simply about to become the world champs. We had wanted it, worked for it, and believed we could do it. No one had been afraid to play, to take risks, to pay the price. This was going to be sweet.

With a runner on, the *A's* fans still believed. The noise was deafening, taking on a personality of its own. When Tony Phillips came to the plate, Terry Steinbach moved to the on-deck circle, prepared to hit for Walt Weiss. I wanted to end it right then so I wouldn't have to face the tying run. I decided to ignore the runner and pitch from a wind up. Phillips had singled, struck out, walked, set up one run, and scored another. I overthrew and started him off with a ball. Lansford realized we weren't even paying attention to him, so he stole second on the next pitch without drawing a throw. Ball two.

All I cared about was making sure Steinbach didn't get to the plate. I had seen him homer in the all-star game. He was capable of anything. On ball three, Lansford moved to third. I had struggled in the eighth, and now I was really in trouble in the ninth. I took my time and regrouped.

I worked back up to a full count, with Phillips taking all the way. Lansford edged up the line from third. I wound and fired. He swung. Strike three!

Vin Scully said that like the 1969 Mets, it was the impossible dream revisited. There was no time to kneel, but I raised my eyes and sneaked in a prayer of thanks. We had done it. We had won the World Series.

☆☆☆

It was on a warm September night in Scottsdale, Arizona, during my minor league career, when, alone in my hotel room, I began reading the Gideon Bible. I was searching for answers to the questions that had plagued me ever since my teammate Butch Wickensheimer had begun witnessing to me about Jesus Christ.

Do I believe in God? I asked myself. Do I believe the Bible is God's message to man? Do I believe what the Bible says, that all have sinned, that nothing I can do can save me from my sin, that Jesus already did it for me and that He is the only way to God? Do I want Christ in my life? Do I want to become a Christian?

When I realized that the answer to all my questions was *yes*, I slipped off my bed and knelt beside it.

"God," I prayed, "I don't know everything about You. I don't think I ever will. But I know I'm a sinner and I know I want to be forgiven. I know I want Christ in my life, and I want to go to heaven. I want to become a Christian. With that, I accept You. Amen."

Almost immediately, God gave me a genuine love and compassion for people. I could be happy for someone else without suffering myself. God impressed upon me that He would take care of me and love me no matter what. Whether I made the big leagues and became rich and famous and had everything the world has to offer or I failed at baseball, He would be there.

And that, after all, is what it's all about.

*Adapted from *Out of the Blue* by Orel Hershiser with Jerry B. Jenkins (Brentwood, Tennessee: Wolgemuth & Hyatt, 1989). Used by permission.

NO SECOND STRING

by Garth Jax

☆ **Garth Jax** ☆

GARTH JAX (Football)

- MVP, Most Improved Player—
  Florida State University
- Co-captain, FSU 1985
- Led team in sacks, FSU 1985
- Nominated to Pro Bowl 1986, 1988, 1989
- Played with:
    Dallas Cowboys 1986-1989
    Phoenix Cardinals (current)

*"I want others to look at me and say,
'If Garth Jax can make it, so can I!'"*

I'D BEEN A LOSER ALL MY LIFE, AND SPORTS WAS NO EXception. I was good—but never quite good enough.

"You'll never make it, Garth. You just don't have what it takes." Words from my past echoed in my head over and over again. Now, at the end of my college career, those words came back to haunt me once more. Was it true? Would I be drafted by the NFL or would I end up a loser once again?

No, I decided. I would not listen to those words anymore. Only months earlier, I had come to know Jesus. Now I had a heavenly Father, and He told me I was not a loser, that through Him, I could do anything. I claimed that promise and I waited.

I was drafted by the Dallas Cowboys, and my faith that God had a purpose and a plan for my life was renewed. However, after an outstanding rookie year, which included being nominated to the Pro Bowl, I was cut from the team.

Had I been wrong? Had my dream of playing professional football been just that—a dream and nothing more? Deep down, I had been so sure....

Five days later, the Cowboys called me back. I went on and played two more years for them; then, last year, I was a starter on the team.

Now, of course, I've been traded to the Phoenix Cardinals, and I'm excited to see what God is going to do in my career with this new team. But wherever I spend my professional career, one thing I will always remember—there is no second string on God's team. We may not all be superstars in the eyes of the world. We may be called to work in the background, to encourage those in the limelight. That's okay. So long as we remember that "whatever you do, whether in word or deed, do it all in the name of the Lord Jesus, giving thanks to God the Father through him" (Col. 3:17).

☆☆☆

I grew up in what I call a "conditional" family. I was constantly striving to achieve approval—and never quite getting it. We were a religious family, but none of us had a relationship with Jesus Christ. Consequently, I grew up with a twisted view of life.

By the time I was in the seventh grade, my parents had divorced and I had begun experimenting with drugs—searching for some sort of identity, some sort of purpose. Before long, I had tried everything—sex, drugs, rock-and-roll—and I found nothing but frustration, loneliness and heartache.

Finally, a junior in high school, I tried suicide. I took about 25 pills, drank a six-pack of beer, and waited to die. When that didn't work, I loaded a gun and pointed it at my head. Just as I was about to pull the trigger, my brother came along and stopped me.

But it was only a temporary reprieve. Over the next few years, I attempted suicide several times—only to fail repeatedly. I also tried several different personal relationships. None of them worked out, either.

Then, on June 21, 1985, I woke up and said to myself, "Garth, you've tried it all—drugs, women, alcohol. None of them was the answer. You've got to try something else."

I got on my knees and prayed, "God, I don't know what you have to offer me, but I'm so miserable, I just want out of all this!"

That's when I felt God's assurance that the peace and joy and acceptance I'd been seeking all my life was right there. He was the answer.

My life began that day. I learned what it truly is to be a man. And God has reinforced that many times throughout the years. I have faced countless "giants" since then, just as I had before I knew Him. The difference is that now, like David, I have the faith and the power to defeat those giants. And I have learned that, so long as I keep my eyes on the Giver rather than on the gifts, the blessings will continue to come.

FATHERLY PROMOTION

by Veronica Karaman

☆ **Veronica Karaman** ☆

Photo used with permission.

VERONICA KARAMAN (Golf)

- Woman's Western Golf Foundation Scholarship 1977-1981
- Regional All-American 1979
- Duke Univ. Athletic Association Scholarship 1977-1981
- Played:
  Duke Univ. 1977-1981
  (captain, senior year)
  Women's Professional Golf Tour 1982
  Tampa Bay Mini-Tour 1982
  Future's Golf Tour 1988

"It is so important not to confuse the prizes of this world with God's prize, which is Jesus Himself. He alone is the imperishable wreath, the trophy at the end of the race, the One who makes all of our discipline and training and sacrifices worthwhile."

M Y FATHER, WHOSE LOVE FOR GOLF FIRST KINDLED within me that same passion for the game, died when I was 15. At a time when any girl seriously considering a professional golfing career most needs a father's guidance and training, I found myself without the source of motivation and support I so desperately longed for. Looking back, however, I see how miraculously my heavenly Father stepped in to fulfill that role. So many instances illustrate His faithfulness to me, but one time in particular stands out in my memory.

I was 16 years old and playing a practice round at Oakmont East, a "less than desirable" course, which just happens to be adjacent to one of the most renowned courses in the country, Oakmont Country Club. It was hot and crowded, and as I looked ahead of me, I saw that the cart two groups in front of me had only two people in it—a man and a woman. I decided that if I could get past the first group to that couple, I might be able to put my bag on their cart and join them. I was more than slightly relieved when, after working my way up to them, they agreed.

As we crested the top of a hill, I looked down on the Oakmont East course and realized that the vast, lush expanse of the Oakmont Country Club course was also visible from that hill. "Wow!" I exclaimed. "Would I ever love to play there someday!"

"Well, honey," the woman said, turning to me, "did you know that you're playing with the manager of that course?" Before I knew it, they had taken me to Oakmont Country Club and given me a job in the golf shop, which enabled me to play and practice on one of the finest courses in the country. A door of opportunity had opened to me that I could never have opened myself. It was only one of many times I experienced God's

"Fatherly promotion" during the course of my career.

☆☆☆

Although I became a Christian during my junior year of college, my struggle to lead a victorious Christian life continued for several years after that. Golf seemed to be more my god than Jesus, because it was performance and success in golf that determined my emotional state, my physical and mental well-being, my pursuits, my sacrifices, my everyday choices in life. I knew that was wrong, but I couldn't seem to reconcile my dedication to golf and my dedication to God, so in 1982 I decided to give up golf completely. It was an incredibly difficult decision, because everything I knew myself to be was based on golf. Just before I gave up the sport, however, something happened that planted a seed of hope within me, a seed that would lie dormant for years, but would eventually burst forth with promise.

I was visiting a friend of mine who was preparing for a tournament. I had always considered her an average player, not quite on a level with my own abilities and talents. As I observed her praying and fasting and seeking God for victory in the upcoming tournament, I was bothered. I had never considered praying for a win to be a valid request. But when she went out the next day and literally wiped out the "cream of the crop" players, it blew me away! I realized that God had honored my friend because she had honored Him. I knew then that if He would do that for her, He would also do it for me.

Still, I was determined to leave golf behind, and for five years I did just that, devoting myself entirely to academic rather than athletic pursuits. Throughout that time, however, the memory of my friend's victory nagged at me, and I would find myself praying, "Lord, if the same power that raised Jesus Christ from the dead truly lives inside of me, I want you to resurrect my golf game."

In September of 1987, I went out to lunch with some friends. One of them asked me, "Veronica, what do you *really* want to do? What is the *real* desire of your heart?"

At that point, I confided to them that I had a dream of winning the U.S. Open for the glory of Jesus Christ. My friends became very excited for me and began to pray. And things began to happen.

The next thing I knew, I had a sponsor and I was back out playing golf again. But in July 1988, while playing the third hole at the Manhattan Country Club, I looked down and saw two balls instead of one. I felt like I was going to collapse. For the first time in my life, I was forced to withdraw from competition.

Things went from bad to worse. I learned I had a virus similar to mononucleosis, and I was bedridden for an entire month, followed by a six-month recovery period. During that time, my agreement with my sponsor was terminated and my golf instructor was tragically killed in a plane crash. Once again, I was seriously questioning God as to whether or not I should continue on with golf. And yet I believed with all my heart that when the time came for me to quit, it would be on a positive note, not a negative one. So, with little or no desire, inspiration or motivation, I resolved to go on.

As always, God was faithful, miraculously providing for my every need. In June 1989, after not having played in a tournament for an entire year, I tied for first place in the U.S. Open Qualifier in Dallas, Texas.

Going on to the U.S. Open, I didn't make the cut, but I experienced the unconditional love of God during that tournament as I never had before. I just couldn't get down and defeated about my performance.

In the past I had performed in order to feel good about myself, both as an athlete and as a Christian. This time, I knew that God had brought me to the U.S. Open for a higher purpose. Just before arriving at the Open, He had led me to write a tract about the good news of Jesus Christ and to distribute copies to every player and every spectator I came in contact with. I even felt impressed by God to write a personal note to each of the 150 women golfers involved in the tournament, and then to leave those notes, along with my tracts, on their lockers.

Although my dream to win the Open had not been realized, I felt nothing but joy as I walked off the last green, because even though I hadn't won the tournament, I had won something so much greater—a new dimension and a deeper sense of God's victorious love.

MAKING A CHOICE

by Joe King

☆ **Joe King** ☆

JOE KING (Football, Weight-lifting, Track and Field)

- All-Area, Litchfield High School (track and field)
- Most Improved Offensive Lineman, Univ. of Alabama 1986
- Set two weight-lifting records, Univ. of Alabama
- Played with
  Cincinnati Bengals 1989
- Wife: Tracey

*"I always felt I had so much to prove to so many people
—the people back home in Gadsden, Alabama, my
family and friends. Everything I did, right or wrong,
was for all the wrong reasons."*

FOOTBALL HAS BEEN IMPORTANT TO ME SINCE I WAS eight or nine years old and played in the PeeWee League. Because of my size—I'm now 6'7" and weigh 310 pounds—I was a natural. The trouble was, even though I was big, people said I wasn't aggressive or mean enough to be successful at the game. But at the end of my sophomore year of high school, I was offered a football scholarship to the University of Alabama. I figured that should show everybody!

My "success" went right to my head. The stress associated with football created a lot of problems for me. I thought I could just kick back and coast into success. I drank my way through the last two years of high school and right into college, sure that I was in control of my drinking and could still succeed at football.

I started in my first game as a sophomore in 1986 against Ohio State. It was a good season, but my drinking was beginning to catch up to me. The last game of the year—the Sun Bowl—I was suspended because of drinking-related problems.

When Coach Bill Curry came in the next season, he offered me a fresh start. I played well, but the drinking continued and I was suspended for three games during the season. At the end of the year, the coach gave me an ultimatum: "If you want to stay on the team, you've got to get treatment."

There it was, in black and white. I couldn't have it both ways. I couldn't continue drinking and still have a successful career in football. I had to choose. It was one or the other—not both.

I have learned now that no matter what it is you want to succeed in, whether it's sports or something else entirely, you have to make a choice. If you continue in destructive habits, they will eventually ruin your career—and your life, too.

☆☆☆

I grew up in Gadsden, Alabama, in a wonderful Christian home, and accepted the Lord when I was 12 years old. Things went well for me until I was about 16. That's when I was offered a football scholarship to the University of Alabama, and I started drinking.

By the time I got to college, the drinking had led to cocaine—"crack." That stuff is so powerful, it took me about three seconds to get hooked. When a random urine test in 1987 turned up positive for cocaine use, I was released from the team.

Out of money and desperate for alcohol and drugs, I drove through the ghettos of Birmingham late one night, hoping to score some crack. When I stopped my car and two guys came over to offer me a sale, I couldn't get away because they climbed in the car with me. When they tried to rob me and found I had no money, they put a .38 to my head and said, "You're going to die."

I ended up in the hospital recuperating from a gunshot wound that narrowly missed my spinal cord, but *still* I hadn't reached bottom. Even though I knew God had spared my life, I continued drinking and using cocaine. It wasn't until I stood in court facing a judge on a hit-and-run charge that I finally reached my turning point.

Checking myself into a treatment program for five months, I allowed God to begin dealing with me, teaching me, leading me. I realized how blessed I was that my wife, Tracy, had stayed with me through all my problems. I also realized how blessed I was that Jesus still loved me through it all.

In the summer of 1989 I signed with the Cincinnati Bengals. I was playing well, but made the difficult decision to leave the team when I realized that I wasn't yet strong enough to handle the money that comes with playing in the pros. With God's help, I will be able to handle those pressures someday soon and go back to playing the game of football once again. But whatever my future holds, the most important thing to me is that it be God's will.

In the meantime, I'm staying clean. I attend support meetings, read my Bible and go to church faithfully. And, although I still struggle with past memories, I praise God every day that I am alive and have a chance to serve Him.

SOMETHING NEW AND WONDERFUL

by Tom Landry

☆ **Tom Landry** ☆

Photo courtesy of the Dallas Cowboys; used with permission.

TOM LANDRY (Football)
- All-Southwest Conference 1947
- All-Pro 1954
- Played with:
  New York Yankees 1949
  New York Giants 1950-1955
- Asst. Defensive Coach, New York Giants 1956-1959
- Head Coach, Dallas Cowboys 1960-1988
- Wife: Alicia
- Children: Tom, Jr., Kitty, Lisa

"As a Christian I know my life is in God's hands. He has a plan for me. Therefore, I never worry about tomorrow and try to keep winning and losing and the good and bad things that happen in my life in perspective. The knowledge that my life is in God's hands helps me keep my composure or regain it in tough situations."[1]

W HEN Roger Staubach came to me and told me about the plans for a "Tom Landry Day," I couldn't imagine why anyone would want go to all the trouble to plan such a thing. In fact, my wife, Alicia, and I both wondered if anybody would even bother to come.

But they did come—approximately 50,000 people!—standing along the streets of Dallas to watch the parade in my honor. There were speeches from such dignitaries as Texas Governor Bill Clements and Dallas Mayor Annette Strauss; telegrams from President George Bush and Billy Graham; and tributes from former Cowboy players, including Roger Staubach.

As Alicia and I rode along the parade route atop that beautiful blue 1954 Buick Skylark convertible, I thought back over the many victories and triumphs God had blessed me with during my coaching career, and I knew none could compare with what I was experiencing at that very moment. I felt so honored—and yet, so humbled—by the outpouring of love from the surrounding crowds.

"We love you, Tom!" they cried, over and over again. "We love you!" The words echoed in my ears and in my heart, reminding me once again of the peace and assurance that had so filled me from the moment I first realized that my 29-year coaching career was now at an end.

Although I would no longer be a football coach, I was still God's child, and I knew beyond a shadow of a doubt that, although the door was closing on that chapter of my life, He had something new and wonderful in store for me just around the bend....

☆☆☆

From the time I was a young boy, attending church was a normal part of my routine. If anyone had asked me, I would have told them I was a Christian, because I really thought I was. But in 1958, I found out otherwise.

A friend of mine, Frank Phillips, invited me to a breakfast meeting, where a group of men got together pretty regularly to read and discuss the Bible. I have to admit, I was a little skeptical, but I decided to give it a try.

When we got to the Melrose Hotel where the meetings were held, there were four tables all set up with about eight or ten men at each one. The Bible discussions began right after breakfast.

Since I always tend to approach things scientifically, I sat back and listened to what these men were saying. By the time the meeting was over, I felt challenged enough to return the next week—and the next. Before long, I found myself wondering about the importance of football in the overall scheme of things. When I realized that, in spite of my successful career and my wonderful family, there was still something missing in my life, I began to wonder if that "something" was Jesus Christ.

One Scripture in particular really nagged at me. It was Matthew 7:24-25, which says, "Therefore whosoever heareth these sayings of mine, and doeth them, I will liken him unto a wise man, which built his house upon a rock: And the rain descended, and the floods came, and the winds blew, and beat upon that house; and it fell not: for it was founded upon a rock" (*KJV*). All of a sudden, I found myself questioning the foundation upon which I had built my own life. And more and more, I was drawn to this Man, Jesus Christ.

It was sometime during the spring of 1959 when I

finally realized that my questions had disappeared, and a feeling of joy had taken their place. I had made the decision. I was committed to follow Jesus Christ. No longer was I simply a church-goer, I was truly a Christian. Since that time, He has been the source of power and love and self-control for my life that I would never have had otherwise.

Note
1. Taken from *The Landry Legend: Grace Under Pressure* by Bob St. John (Dallas, Texas: Word Books, 1989).

THE RIGHT TIME

by Zephaniah "Zeph" Lee

☆ **"Zeph" Lee** ☆

Photo courtesy of the Los Angeles Raiders; used with permission.

"ZEPH" LEE (Football)

- Running back with USC 1981-1985
- Running back with Los Angeles Raiders 1986-1987
- Running back with Denver Broncos 1987
- Defensive back/safety with L.A. Raiders (current)

"I used to think that if I trusted God and worked hard, eventually I would get everything I wanted. The problem was, I didn't realize that everything I wanted wasn't always good for me."

I'D BEEN SPENDING A LOT OF TIME ON THE BENCH, WHEN what I wanted more than anything was to be out on the field with the rest of my team, the Los Angeles Raiders. But when people said to me, "It's not fair, Zeph. You should be out there playing," I did my best not to listen. I knew if I did, I would start complaining.

Now, sitting on the sidelines during a Monday night game while the Denver Broncos ran up the score to 24-0 in the first half, I knew there were going to be some angry people in the locker room at halftime. I was right.

But as some of the others screamed and cursed and called each other names, I sat alone and prayed. It was then that God showed me that He didn't care one bit about how the game turned out. What He did care about was me—and every other player—not only on the Raiders, but on the Broncos, as well. That's when my attitude changed and I began to see, through God's eyes, what was really important.

Then, during the second half of the game, Stacy Toran, our starting safety, went down with an injury. Suddenly, I found myself out on the field.

Having played for the Broncos in the past, I had great respect for their quarterback, John Elway. When he leaned back and threw that ball and I realized it was headed straight for me, I was shocked. Several people who saw the instant replay said that my lips were moving the whole time the ball was sailing through the air toward me. They thought I was scared. Actually, I was praying.

I caught that ball, and it set up the winning field goal. The final score was the Raiders, 27; Broncos, 24. I was given a game ball when it was all over.

I learned a lot that night. I learned that, like it says

in Ecclesiastes 9:12, "Man does not know his time" *(NASB).* Only God knows His appointed time. And only His appointed time is the right time.

☆☆☆

Even though most people call me "Zeph," I've always felt good about being named Zephaniah because I learned that it meant "protected or hidden in a secret place by the Lord." I figure that's a pretty good place to be.

Actually, I came to know the Lord at a young age, thanks to the influence of my grandfather. I lived with my grandparents for a while when I was growing up, and they insisted I go to church every Sunday. When the other kids were outside playing football, I was inside reading the Bible—the *King James Version*—and not really understanding what I was reading. But my grandfather believed what the Bible says in Proverbs 22:6: "Train a child in the way he should go, and when he is old he will not turn from it." By the time I was in high school, I had grown to respect my grandfather and to listen to the things he told me.

But it was when I was in college that a friend confronted me with the Scriptures and asked, "Zeph, are you *really* walking with the Lord?" The more I looked at the verses he showed me, the more I realized I hadn't been walking with the Lord at all—I'd been crawling!

That's when I made the commitment to really walk the walk. As I did, I discovered a new power. Things began to happen in my life. Good things. Not always the way I wanted things to happen, but the way God knew things should happen.

The most important thing I've learned as I walked closer with God was that our situations or circumstances aren't really important. It's what we do while we're in those situations and circumstances that makes a difference. If we spend our time complaining, God can't use us. But if we let God use us right where we are to touch another person—or maybe 10 other people—then those 10 people can move out and touch 10 more people, and on and on.

And that's my contribution to the world—to pour out my life for Christ, just like He did for me.

IMITATION: THE GREATEST FORM OF FLATTERY

by Meadowlark Lemon

MEADOWLARK LEMON
(Basketball)

- Played with:
  Harlem Globetrotters 1954-1978
  Bucketeers 1980-1983
  Shooting Stars (current)

"Although I had occasionally attended church, I had never really heard the Word of God. I just sort of 'checked in' with Jesus at Christmas and Easter. The only time I spoke the word 'Lord' was when I was in trouble."

I'VE HEARD IT SAID THAT IMITATION IS THE GREATEST FORM of flattery. If that's so, then I suppose I should be very proud of having been a member of the most famous basketball team in the world—the Harlem Globetrotters. We were so well known that countries at war actually declared temporary truces when we came to play, starting up again as soon as we left.

When we first went in to some of these countries, they knew very little about the game of basketball but they were anxious to learn. They would come and watch us, then set up their own leagues and begin to imitate our style. Over the years, some of these teams have improved so much that they are actually competing against U.S. teams. In fact, Russia has beaten us twice now.

Looking back on the influence we had on those other teams has taught me a lot about the importance of setting a good example for others to follow. When I first became a Christian in 1982, it was dedicated Christian athletes like Rosey Grier who set the example for me. I have never forgotten the influence of Rosey and others like him, and now I seek to set that same kind of godly example for others who may be watching me, looking for someone to imitate.

☆☆☆

I didn't come to know the Lord in a church like most people. Instead, I met Jesus in a very unusual place—a fashion design studio in Hollywood.

It was April 1982. I was at home in Bel Air, California, when the Lord spoke audibly to me and told me to call a young Jewish girl I knew named Heidi. As I stood there in my home carrying on a discussion with

Someone I couldn't see, I was sure I was losing my mind. But I decided to call my friend anyway.

When Heidi heard my voice, she told me to come right over to her studio. I did, and found a preacher there with her. He explained that he didn't know what he was doing at the studio except that the Lord had directed him to come there at that particular time. Then Heidi asked if they could pray with me.

I agreed, and we went into her small office in back of the studio, where we prayed the sinner's prayer together. Then they read a Scripture to me from the Bible—Romans 10:9,10:

That if you confess with your mouth, "Jesus is Lord," and believe in your heart that God raised him from the dead, you will be saved. For it is with your heart that you believe and are justified, and it is with your mouth that you confess and are saved.

In the back room of a fashion design studio in Hollywood, I heard the Word of God for the first time, and I knew my life would never be the same again.

ALWAYS A BRIDESMAID...

by Bob Lilly

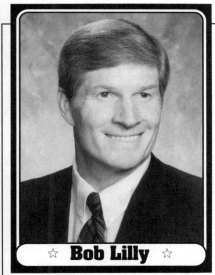

☆ **Bob Lilly** ☆

BOB LILLY (Football)

- All Southwest Conference (two years)
- All-American (senior year)
- All-Pro (seven years)
- Pro Bowl (11 years)
- Defensive tackle with Dallas Cowboys 1961-1975
- Wife: Ann
- Children: Bob, Jr., Michelle, Christienne, Mark

"Even though I knew better, when I got into college, I went with the crowd because I had no standard to live up to. That's why young people today are having so many problems. There's no standard for them to follow."

I PLAYED ALL 14 YEARS OF MY PRO-FOOTBALL CAREER with the Dallas Cowboys under Coach Tom Landry. Some of my best memories—and some of my worst—are from that period of time.

Probably the worst time I can remember was when we played St. Louis on a Monday night and they beat us 38-0. Believe me, it doesn't get much worse than that. But the funny thing was, we went on to play in the Super Bowl that same year!

As usual, though, we ended up being the "brides-maid," rather than the "bride." We lost. It seemed the Cowboys were good enough to almost make it—but not quite. Until the following year, that is.

It was January 1972 and, once again, we were head-ed for the Super Bowl in New Orleans to compete against the Miami Dolphins. Winning the Super Bowl is the ultimate goal of every football player, and this year we were determined.

It was a no-nonsense trip. All business, no fun. But it paid off. We worked hard and we won. At long last, we had become the bride, rather than just the brides-maid. As we carried a smiling Coach Landry off the field, we knew we had put the Dallas Cowboys on the map.

☆☆☆

Even though I was raised with strong Christian guide-lines and principles, I strayed away during my college and pro-football days because I had no biblical stan-dard to guide me. But the reason I didn't stray any fur-ther than I did was because of a very special person who did indeed have biblical standards, and who al-ways lived up to them.

I'll never forget my first rookie meeting with the

Dallas Cowboys. Coach Tom Landry, who had become a Christian just two years before I joined the team in 1961, stood up in front of us and outlined his priorities in life: God first, family second, and the team third. By the time he was through talking, most of us rookies thought we had landed in the wrong place, because Coach Landry obviously had his priorities mixed up.

But throughout my 14 years with the Cowboys, Coach Landry—a very organized and disciplined individual—never deviated from the biblical standards that guided his life. He incorporated them into his team strategies, held prayer meetings and quoted occasional Scripture verses in a way that made them seem relevent to football.

But I didn't really come to know the Lord until some time after my pro-football career had ended. I was in the midst of a successful business venture, but my marriage was falling apart at the seams. Then, my wife, Ann, became a born-again believer.

I thought she was crazy. Everytime I came home, I'd find her watching Christian TV, listening to Christian tapes or reading the Bible. And she was so sweet and good to me! It took awhile, but I finally came to the point of saying, "Honey, I'm at the end of my rope. I know now that you love me. You're the light of my life, and I just want what you've got."

Ann then took me to see a blind evangelist who explained salvation to me and introduced me to Jesus Christ, all through the use of his Braille Bible, which he had basically memorized in its entirety! But through his words, and through listening to the New Testament tapes several times, I eventually caught the vision of the Great Commission, and my life has never been the same.

Those same biblical standards that had so inspired me in Coach Tom Landry over the years had become my standards, as well.

☆ **Jo Jo Starbuck** ☆

See page 199

FINDING MY SOURCE OF CONFIDENCE

by Lamar Lundy

☆ **Lamar Lundy** ☆

Photo used with permission.

LAMAR LUNDY (Football)

- Member of most honored line in pro-football: "Fearsome Foursome," Los Angeles Rams
- Tight end/defensive right end L.A. Rams 1957-1969
- Wife: Patricia
- Children: Lamar III, Ronald, Vicki, Tara

"Because of my football career, I spent a lot of years handing out autographs to kids. But now I truly have something worthwhile to give them, and that's Jesus Christ."

I GRADUATED FROM HIGH SCHOOL IN RICHMOND, Indiana, then went on to play football at Purdue University. From there I was drafted by the Los Angeles Rams in 1957, where I played for 13 years. Along with Rosey Grier, Deacon Jones and Merlin Olsen, I became part of one of the most famous defensive lines in the history of football—the Fearsome Foursome.

Although my football career holds many fond memories for me, one game in particular stands out as the most exciting. I believe it was in 1967. We were playing the St. Louis Cardinals, and it seemed that everything was going my way. I made several tackles, got to the quarterback a few times, and came away feeling very encouraged about my abilities on the football field. But none of it begins to compare to what I experienced when I accepted Jesus Christ as my Lord and Savior. It was only as a direct result of knowing Him that I finally found my true source of confidence and assurance.

☆☆☆

Although my mother saw to it that I attended church as a boy, I never made any sort of commitment to God. I suppose I was always somewhat aware of Him, but I didn't know Him at all. In fact, I went through my entire football career before I finally came to a point of turning my life over to Jesus Christ.

I had experienced some problems with a thyroid condition and diabetes during my career, but had been able to deal with those problems and continue playing football. When I was struck with a progressively debilitating muscle disease known as myasthenia gravis, however, I suddenly found myself bedridden, hooked up to a respirator, my eyes taped shut, unable to move any part of my body. I was completely helpless, dependent on others for everything. I felt like my brain was in prison, because it was the only part of me that was functioning on its own.

During that time my wife encouraged me to give my life to the Lord. Unable to speak, I prayed silently in my heart. Soon after that, things began to change. It took about four years to progress to the point where I was once more self-reliant, but as I moved toward that point, I also moved away from my dependence on God. By the end of that four-year recovery period, I was back to thinking I could do things myself—without God's help.

This went on for 10 years. Then, just as I was beginning to experience some financial and personal problems, Rosey Grier came back into my life, asking me to turn everything over to the Lord. Now, Rosey had always been a good friend and I was glad to see him again, but his constant talk about Jesus made me very uncomfortable. On more than one occasion, I know I said things to him that weren't very nice. But being the type of person Rosey is, he kept coming around, encouraging me no matter what I said to him.

Thanks to Rosey's faithfulness and the Lord's continual working within me, I eventually came to a point of making a real commitment to Jesus Christ. I turned it all over to Him—and this time I didn't try to take it back. I have never regretted that decision, and have seen God's goodness and blessings in my life many times since then.

A DREAM COME TRUE

by "Pistol Pete" Maravich

☆ **"Pistol Pete"** ☆

"PISTOL PETE" MARAVICH
(Basketball—deceased)

- Three-time All-American (LSU)
- NCAA records include:
    Highest average in a season (44.5)
    Most points scored in a season
    (1,381)
    Most points scored in a career
    (3,667)
- Inducted into Memorial Basketball Hall of Fame 1987
- During career played with:
    Atlanta Hawks; New Orleans Jazz; Utah Jazz; Boston Celtics
- Wife: Jackie
- Children: Jaeson, Joshua

"Press Maravich had a dream of what basketball and basketball players could become one day, and his greatest desire was to help me become the realization of his vision. He gave to me his years of knowledge and experience, as well as the ultimate gift—a life dedicated to helping me become the best basketball player I could possibly be."

I HAD HEARD ABOUT THIS SHRINE FOR BASKETBALL LEG-
ends since I was 10 years old. My dad, Press, had
spoken the names of the old-timers reverently, as
though they were departed family members. Now,
gazing at the Memorial Basketball Hall of Fame, I felt
my stomach flutter and throat tighten. Today, the final
scene of Dad's dream would unfold when I slipped the
gold ring on my finger and stood in the hall of champions. How I wished he were by my side.

Just five years earlier, playing with the Celtics in
nearby Boston, it seemed the dream had died after another afternoon of dribbling, passing, and shooting a
basketball on a hardwood floor. The final horn had
blown on a green and white intrasquad game. The
team had looked good, and the guys were pumped up
as we came into the Celtic locker room. I had played
well, scoring 38 points. Other players were whooping
and laughing, but I had to force a smile.

Nearly 25 years had passed since Dad had handed
me his vision of winning a championship ring. He had
always wanted me to play on a winning team and be
recognized as the best in the world. But through all the
record-breaking years in high school and at LSU, and
despite being a three-time all-American, player-of-the-
year, NCAA all-time leading scorer, and spending a
decade in the pros, winning a championship had elud-
ed me. I couldn't get that ring!

This is what my dad had wanted for me. But he
would just have to understand my decision. I had
managed to score nearly 16,000 points in pro basketball, but the NBA had worn me out physically. And
worse than any physical ailments, along the way I had
picked up an attitude that can ruin any athlete—the
wrong kind of pride.

I dried off and dressed. Slowly I dug through the locker and filled my gym bag with what now seemed to be the relics of my entire life. I couldn't find the words to tell anybody that this was it; the "Pistol" had fired his last shot. The diamond ring would be on someone else's finger. What would Dad say when I told him that his dream, the dream that had become Pistol Pete, was dead?

Waiting to hear my name called at the Hall of Fame, I knew I had been wrong that day five years ago. Dad's dream had come true....

My father became a symbol of what love and compassion can do in anyone's life, and I am happy to accept that love as his heir to a dream.

☆☆☆

It was a cool November evening in 1982, with a chilling wind blowing across Lake Pontchartrain. My conscience was bothering me as never before.

I recalled the night I had taken my first drink on the steps of the church, and how that first sip nearly ruined my life. I considered the effect it had on my mother and on our family in general. I remembered all the ugly things I'd done to people, and I recalled the friends and enemies I had made in college and in the pros. My thoughts wandered to all the rebellion I had toward God, my family, and others. All the horrible things I had said and the stupid things I had done seemed to be illuminated. No matter how hard I tried, I couldn't derail the thoughts.

Finally, I recognized that it was more than just thoughts running through my head. It was sin.

I cried out to God, saying, "I've cursed you and I've spit on you. I've mocked you and used your name in vain. I've kicked, punched, and laughed at you. Oh, God, can you forgive me, can you forgive me? Please, save me, please. I've had it with this life of mine. I've had it with all the world's answers for happiness. All of it, the money, fame, and things have left me so empty."

Suddenly, without warning, I heard a voice say, "Be strong. Lift thine own heart." The voice seemed to reverberate throughout the room. What I'd heard hadn't come from within me. It was an audible voice!

I prayed a simple prayer as best I could. "Jesus Christ, come into me life...forgive me of my sin. I believe with all my heart that you died for me and rose from the grave so I would have eternal life. Make me the person you want me to be."

Through this simple act of surrender, the void that once loomed so large was filled. From that moment on, my life was never to be the same.

*Adapted from *Heir to a Dream* by Pete Maravich and Darrel Campbell (Nashville, Tennessee: Thomas Nelson, Inc., 1987). Used by permission.

COUNTING IT ALL LOSS

by Scott McGregor

☆ **Scott McGregor** ☆

SCOTT McGREGOR (Baseball)

- 20-game winner 1980
- All-Star Game 1981
- Member of 1983 World Champion Baltimore Orioles
- Played with New York Yankees 1972-1976
- Pitcher with Baltimore Orioles 1976-1988
- Wife: Cara
- Children: Eric, Katie, Michael

"Now that my baseball career is behind me and I'm in the ministry, I find that working with and helping these kids is so much more challenging than playing baseball could ever be!"

ALOT OF WONDERFUL THINGS HAPPENED TO ME IN MY baseball career, particularly during the five years after I accepted the Lord in 1979. I became known as the "winningest" pitcher in baseball, winning 75-80 games during that five-year period. I played in two World Series, as well as on the All-Star team. But the highlight of those years had to be that night in Philadelphia in 1983—the night before the final game of the World Series.

As I lay there, tossing and turning and trying to sleep, I alternately experienced joy and excitement one minute, panic and tension the next. I knew that if I was going to get any sleep at all that night, I desperately needed to find a sense of peace for my jumbled emotions. And so I turned to the Prince of Peace Himself, Jesus Christ.

Searching the Scriptures, I felt led to read the third chapter of Philippians, where the Apostle Paul lists his human accomplishments and "pedigree," so to speak. In other words, he was born in the right place to the right family, had the right education, did all the right things—and yet, he says, "I also count all things loss...that I may gain Christ" (v. 8, *NKJV*).

That's me! I realized. *That passage of Scripture could be talking about me!* Because in spite of having grown up with all the opportunities any child could ever want, in spite of the many successes I had already experienced in my career, none of it would make a bit of difference when it came down to where I would spend eternity. The only thing that would matter then would be my relationship with Jesus.

I was able to sleep peacefully after that, then went out on the mound the next day and pitched one of my very best games ever. We won the series, and I was elated! But the most exciting thing of all was knowing that the peace within me wasn't dependent on whether or not we won the game. My peace was based on the knowledge that God loved me—and that was the only thing that really counted.

☆☆☆

Athletics has been a central part of my life for as long as I can remember. I grew up in Southern California with a baseball diamond just around the corner. (My dad even teases me that I threw my bottle before I drank it!) Baseball, basketball, football—I played them all, and seemed to have natural abilities for each sport. It was in baseball, however, that I really excelled.

Starring in Little League, Babe Ruth, and finally on my high school baseball team, I was drafted right out of high school by the New York Yankees. My dreams seemed to be coming true at a very early age!

Although I had done a little drinking in my senior year of high school, I always swore I would never get involved with drugs. But now—out in the "real world" with success dangling tantalizingly in front of me—the pressures began to mount. Whereas before my father had always been there to bail me out of my childhood pranks, and my high school principal and teachers had been willing to ignore some of my escapades because of my baseball abilities, suddenly I was on my own—no one to cover for me. And the "big-time" baseball heroes of my youth were now flesh-and-blood people, people whose lives reflected anything but the happiness and success I had assumed was theirs. I mean, these were the guys I had watched and admired on TV, guys who had their pictures on bubble-gum cards, and here they were drinking, doing drugs, stuck in unhappy marriages, breaking bats in fits of rage after losing games—I could hardly believe what I was seeing. And yet, it wasn't long before I found myself joining them, not only in the drinking, but in drugs, as well—the very drugs I had sworn never to use.

In 1976 I was traded to the Orioles. By 1978 my career was in full swing! Not only was I in the starting rotation, I was now known as one of the up-and-coming stars in the major leagues. My wife, Cara, was expecting our first child, we had recently bought our first home, and things were going great, right? Wrong. On the outside it appeared that I had achieved everything I had ever dreamed of or hoped for. On the inside I was frustrated, disillusioned, empty. That's when I started attending Bible studies.

Not long after that, I hurt my elbow. It was the beginning of spring training, 1979, and I was put on the disabled list. That was when I realized how quickly my baseball career could be over.

Still on the disabled list, I stood out in center field one June day in the middle of batting practice and looked up into the heavens. I was thinking about the Bible study I had attended earlier that morning. After the Bible study I had prayed with the pastor, but still didn't really understand what was going on in my life. And so I prayed. "Lord, everything this world painted to be such a great picture just hasn't panned out to be the truth. If You're real, come into my heart and do something with my life."

I've been out of baseball for several years now and am serving the Lord in full-time ministry as a youth pastor. Every day I remind myself that God put me in a position where I became famous, but He also gave me a light to shine. It's a wonderful opportunity and an awesome responsibility, because young people need heroes to look up to, heroes they can count on. But the most important thing to remember is that it's not who I am, but who's in me that makes all the difference.

BECOMING A CHAMPION

by Madeline Manning Mims

☆ **M. Mims** ☆

MADELINE MIMS (Track)

- Gold Medalist: 1967 Pan American Games, setting new American record
- Gold Medalist: 800 meters in the 1968 Olympic Games, Mexico setting a new World record
- Silver Medalist, 400 meters, 1972 Olympics, Munich
- Member of 4 Olympic Teams: 1968, 1972, 1976, 1980
- Ranked #1 in the world by *Track and Field News* in 1967, 1968, 1969
- Held American outdoor record for women's 800 meters for 15 years
- Inducted into the National and Olympic Hall of Fame: 1984
- Husband: Roderick
- Children: John, Lana

"I had these long legs with these big feet on the ends of them, and they were going east and west at the same time. I didn't like Madeline then. I hadn't realized yet that God had made me tall and slim for a purpose."

AS A TEENAGER GROWING UP IN THE GHETTOS OF CLEVE-
land, Ohio, I never dreamed I would someday
be a world champion. I didn't even know what the
Olympic Games were. But when my physical education teacher asked me if I wanted to try out for basketball, volleyball or track, I went out for all three.

Our girls' team was in the running for the state
championship, and we needed someone to run the
440-yard dash. Since I had the longest legs, I was "vol-
unteered." When I asked what I had to do, I was told,
"Just stretch your legs out in front of you." I looked
like an ostrich going around that track!

But I won—in fact, I set a new school record—and
our school won the state championship. On top of that,
a Hungarian coach, Alex Ferenczy, spotted me and decided I had championship qualities.

Alex became more than my coach. He became my
dear friend and a "father figure," besides. He got me
into meets where earlier black athletes had not been
welcome. He fought for my rights as an athlete. He encouraged me. He believed in me. And he rode
me—hard. Harder, I was sure, than any of the other
girls on the team.

I resented that sometimes, and I hated all the work.
But because my mother had taught me at a young age
to submit to those in authority, I obeyed his every com-
mand without question. This caused problems for me
with some of the other girls on the team, but in the
long run it paid off.

Within one year of becoming my coach, Alex saw
me win my first national championship. And he was
there in Mexico City in 1968 to see me win my Gold
Medal.

It wasn't until I got older that I realized how unusual it was for a Hungarian coach to suddenly turn up in the ghettos of Cleveland and take a poor girl like me under his wing. That's when I knew that God's hand had been on me all along—that He had guided and led my career every step of the way.

☆☆☆

I came to know Jesus as my Lord and Savior when I was only six years old. But growing up in the ghetto, I had to fight to overcome the street-mentality that said, "You ain't nothin'. You ain't never gonna be nothin', so you might as well not even try."

Shy and introverted, I never felt like I quite fit in with the other kids. When I would see them up on stage receiving awards for scholastic achievements or art or music, I envied them. I didn't think I had any special talent that would ever be recognized in that way.

But when I returned from Russia with the other American athletes in 1965, I was met at the door of my high school by the principal, who wanted to introduce me to the mayor, who wanted to present me with a key to the city. I was then introduced to the president of the city council, who wanted to read from a long scroll—and they wanted to do all this in front of an assembly of 3,000 people!

As I sat up there on that stage listening to the band play and the speakers speak, watching the cheerleaders jump around, staring out at that sea of faces looking back at me, I just couldn't understand what was going on. Was all of this really for me?

By the time my name was finally called, I had taken the piece of paper containing my speech and crumpled it into a tiny ball. My palms were sweating so badly that, even when I smoothed out the paper, I couldn't read the words. So I went up to the microphone and explained my problem, then went on to talk from my heart.

For 20 minutes the audience laughed and cried, and I realized that they loved me. Me—Madeline Manning! And I knew at that moment that God had allowed me to overcome that mentality that said, "You ain't nothin.' You ain't never gonna be nothin', so why even try." I was somebody because God had made me—just like I was!

THE BEST AND WORST OF TIMES

by Lenny Moore

☆ **Lenny Moore** ☆

LENNY MOORE (Football)

- All-East, All-State, All-American—Penn State
- Baltimore Colts Rookie of the Year 1956
- Member of 10,000-Yard-Plus Club
- NFL record for most consecutive games scoring a TD (18)
- League's MVP (Jim Thorpe Trophy) 1964
- Comeback Player of the Year 1964
- Pro Bowl (seven times)
- All-Pro, All-League (five times)
- Inducted into Pro-Football Hall of Fame 1975
- Wife: Edith
- Children: Lenny, Leslie, Carol, Toni, Terri, Brenda, Ronnie, Ray, Wiley

"I didn't realize it at that time, but there was one man more than all others who spoke of the finer life and whose actions exemplified what he said. Raymond Berry [presently head coach of the New England Patriots] was a candle of hope in that darkened time who gave the promise of light to those of us boxed in and veiled from an even break. In word and deed, he lived the Christian life."

W E HAD A GREAT FOOTBALL SEASON DURING MY SENIOR year of high school, and when the scholarship offers began to roll in, it was the first time I had seriously considered going away to college. No one in our family had attended college before, so I looked forward to my four years at Penn State as a new and exciting experience.

Although those four years provided me with a lot of positive memories, there were also a lot of negative happenings. It was a time of changing social values and unrest, a time when I first became vividly aware of the racial situation in our country. There were certain stadiums where we were not allowed to play, certain social occasions where we were not welcome—all because of the color of our skin. It was depressing and degrading, and it bothered me deeply.

One of the main reasons I was able to persevere in my chosen sport, however, and not succumb to the demoralizing aspects of racial prejudice was the influence and example of a man named Andy Stopper. Andy had been my high school football coach, as well as my friend and mentor. Andy was white.

Although I was looked down on by some whites—only because I was black—I didn't become dissatisfied with whites (as a class) because I would then have been setting myself against Andy—only because he was white! The way Andy Stopper lived his life taught me that each individual must be deserving of every and all considerations that his entire being warrants.

And so I survived the racial skirmishes of my college years and, in 1956, I was the number-one draft pick of the Baltimore Colts. Even at the professional level, however, I continued to experience isolated incidents of racial prejudice. I was hurt by it, but my career went on, climaxing with my induction into the National Football Hall of Fame in 1975, my award being presented to me by none other than my former high school football coach, Andy Stopper!

Anyone would think I'd have been overjoyed and triumphant at having overcome the racial and social barriers I had encountered, but what should have been the best of times, for me seemed to be the worst....

☆☆☆

In 1974 when I received the news that I had been elected to the National Football Hall of Fame, it was a hollow victory. Of course, I was deeply honored, but the news of my induction was overshadowed by the other news I had just received—my dear wife, Erma, to whom I had been married less than a year, had cancer.

Erma was my second wife (my first wife, Frances, and I divorced in 1973, due to my being caught up in my football career and trying to live life the world's way). Although Erma lived long enough to attend my induction on August 2, 1975, she died soon after, on October 16. I felt like I'd lost everything I'd ever worked for or cared about.

I'll never forget walking into my lonely, empty house one day after her death and screaming out in pain, "God! If you can hear me up there, listen, please! Erma, my love, is gone, there's no other love and no other life for me here. Lord, please take my life—I want to die!"

You see, although I'd been raised in a Christian home and baptized at the age of 11, I had never really come to know God personally. I believed in Him, I thanked Him each time I scored a touchdown throughout my career, I even carried a miniature Bible into each game, tucked down inside my right thigh pad. But I just didn't know Him.

I believe God heard my cry of pain, though, because not long after I begged Him to take my life, He sent Edith to me. Not only did Edith eventually become my beloved wife and partner, it was she who led me to the foot of the Cross, bringing me face-to-face with Jesus Christ for the first time.

It was in 1981, as a direct result of Edith's prayers and influence on my life, that I first accepted Jesus Christ. We still had some ups and downs in our marriage, however, because I wanted be a Christian while continuing to hold on to the ways of the world. I didn't realize I had to make a choice.

Then, in 1983, I finally made a real heart commitment to God. Miraculously, the Lord delivered me of my desire for alcohol. He also led me to confess something to Edith that I had previously withheld for fear of losing her. Although Edith was hurt by my confession, God healed her heart and mind, and drew us together even closer than before. Since that time, we have seen many of our friends and family members come to know Jesus Christ, including my son Leslie, whom God delivered from drugs and who remains drug-free to this day.

There is so much more in my heart that I wish I had time and space to share, but the words of my favorite Scripture passage, Phillipians 4:6-9, sum it up best:

> *Be anxious for nothing, but in everything by prayer and supplication, with thanksgiving, let your requests be made known to God; and the peace of God, which surpasses all understanding, will guard your hearts and*

minds through Christ Jesus. Finally, brethren, whatever things are true, whatever things are noble, whatever things are just, whatever things are pure, whatever things are lovely, whatever things are of good report, if there is any virtue and if there is anything praiseworthy—meditate on these things. The things which you learned and received and heard and saw in me, these do, and the God of peace will be with you (NKJV).

Thanks to God's Word and to all He has done in our lives, it truly is the best of times.

TAKING ADVANTAGE OF MY SECOND CHANCE

by Zeke Mowatt

☆ **Zeke Mowatt** ☆

ZEKE MOWATT (Football)

- Currently plays with the New York Giants (eight years)

"I remember one time when somebody asked me, If you die, will you go to heaven? I had a problem answering that question. I figured I'd done some good things in my life, but I just wasn't sure. Now I know."

I CAN'T TELL YOU HOW MANY ATHLETES WITH PROMISING futures have seen their careers ended in a split second because of injuries. In 1985, I could have been one of them.

When I blew my knee out, there were people who thought I would never come back and play football again. But during my recovery from major knee surgery, I learned that it doesn't matter what anybody thinks or says. What matters is being in God's will. And it wasn't God's will for my career to end that soon.

He gave me another chance. Four years later, I'm still playing football. But out of gratitude for that second chance, I try to take every opportunity to use my position as an athlete to tell others about Christ. When people comment on my athletic abilities and talents and successes, I tell them it's not me, it's God. He's the one who blessed me with those talents and abilities, and gave me a second chance to use them for His glory.

☆☆☆

I was raised in a Christian home and attended church regularly. My father was a deacon and my mother a deaconess in our church, and I accepted the Lord at a very young age. But as I continued on in church through my teens, I really didn't realize what it meant to make a true commitment to live for Christ.

When I went off to college, I still believed the things I'd learned as a kid at home and in church, but I didn't live the way I knew I should. I wanted to "fit in" with my friends, so I did a lot of stupid things. It wasn't until I got into professional football with the

New York Giants that I began to understand what being a Christian was really all about.

I met some real committed players on the Giants team, and they began to influence my thinking. Even though I struggled with it for a long time, finally in 1987, I turned my life *completely* over to God. At last I was willing to give up anything and everything that would stand between me and my walk with Christ. I knew it wouldn't be easy, but I've learned to take it one day at a time, and to live by God's promise in Philippians 4:13: "I can do all things through Christ who strengthens me" (*NKJV*).

FARTHER THAN I EVER DREAMED...
by Anthony Muñoz

☆ **Anthony Muñoz** ☆

Photo used with permission.

ANTHONY MUÑOZ (Football)

- Drafted by Cincinnati Bengals (third out of entire draft pick) 1980
- Offensive Lineman of the Year 1989
- Played with:
  USC
- Wife: DeDe
- Children: Michael, Michelle

"During my high school and college days, most everyone thought of me as a 'good' guy, because I was doing so well athletically and behavior-wise. They didn't know about the drinking and the partying, about the things I did just because I wanted to."

HAVING GROWN UP IN SOUTHERN CALIFORNIA, MY ultimate football dream was someday to play in the Rose Bowl. Going into my senior year, even after suffering through and recuperating from two major knee surgeries, I was in the best physical condition ever. Our team was ranked as one of the top teams in the country. The chances of making it to the Rose Bowl looked good.

And then, at our opening game against the Texas Tech Red Raiders in Lubbock, Texas, the game was barely 10 minutes old before I found myself lying on the ground, looking up at the lights of the stadium, writhing in pain from another knee injury. My Rose Bowl dreams seemed to be crashing down around me.

As I began rehabilitation from that third knee surgery, however, I had one main concern—that my team keep winning and go on to the Rose Bowl. If they could do that, I was confident that I could work hard enough to recover in time to join them.

A lot of people thought I was crazy—especially when I started jumping rope with my cast on! But I was determined. Even when our head coach, John Robinson, expressed his concern that I was pushing myself too hard too fast, I knew it was going to be all right.

I didn't miss a practice. My assurance that I would play in the Rose Bowl that year never wavered. And when USC had clinched their spot at the Rose Bowl and their starting line-up was announced, I was in it. After not having played all season, not only was I able to play the entire game—missing no more than a couple of plays—but I also experienced the thrill of beating Ohio State, the number-one ranked team in the country—by a score of 17-16.

My dream had come true. But God wasn't through

blessing me yet. On April 29, 1980, approximately ten minutes after the NFL draft had begun, my phone rang. It was the Cincinnati Bengals, informing me that I had been picked third out of the entire draft (which includes about 12 rounds and 350 players)! I've been with the Bengals ever since.

When I was named Offensive Lineman of the year during halftime ceremonies at the 1989 Pro Bowl, I thanked God for the strength and stamina and endurance He had given me to come so very far—even farther than I had ever dreamed!

☆☆☆

I was right in the middle of a family of five kids—two older brothers, two younger sisters. I never knew my father, but my mother worked hard—sometimes two or three jobs at a time—to provide for us. She was a strong woman, and we respected and loved her.

We had no Bible teaching or church background, however, and it was my freshman year at USC before anyone took the time to explain to me about spiritual things. By that time, I was already heavily into drinking and partying, which had started back in high school. Most people weren't aware of my problem, though, because I continued to excel in sports. But in spite of my life-style, when some of the staff workers from Campus Crusade began talking to me about the Lord, I listened. And I watched. What they said and the way they lived began to have an effect on me.

That summer I began dating a lovely lady named Dede. By Christmas time we were engaged. Although Dede wasn't a Christian, we both found ourselves literally surrounded by people who were. Then, one evening in 1978 after Dede and I were married, we were sitting at the table having dinner with Dede's sister and her husband. Suddenly I realized that, even though I was 6′6″ and weighed 285 pounds, I wasn't strong enough to face the problems of life alone. Up to that time, I had thought my marriage to Dede was the greatest decision I'd ever made. Now I knew it was time for an even greater decision.

As we sat there at the table, both Dede and I prayed and invited Jesus Christ to come into our hearts. And, although we have experienced several trials and tribulations since that time, we know it was the most glorious moment of our lives—more glorious even than playing in the Rose Bowl or the Super Bowl or being named Offensive Lineman of the Year. For all of those honors will someday fade away, but our reign with Christ will go on for all eternity.

"TO WHOM MUCH IS GIVEN..."

by Willie Naulls

☆ **Willie Naulls** ☆

WILLIE NAULLS (Basketball)
- MVP UCLA 1955-1956
- UCLA Single Game Rebounding Record (28)
- NBA All-Star Team (four times)
- MVP New York Knicks (three times)
- NBA World Champion Boston Celtics (three times)
- Inducted into Sportswalk Hall of Fame 1982
- Inducted into UCLA Athletic Hall of Fame 1986
- Played with:
  New York Knickerbockers 1956-1963
  Boston Celtics 1963-1966
- Wife: Anne

"My parents showed me so much love and acceptance while I was growing up that I didn't know we were poor until I took a sociology course at UCLA."

ALTHOUGH I DIDN'T HAVE THE PRIVILEGE OF KNOWING and serving Christ during my athletic career, I can look back now and see how wonderfully God watched over and protected me even then.

Thanks to God's grace and the teaching and guidance of my parents, I grew up thinking enough of myself not to want to set up obstacles to my own success, such as getting involved with drinking or drugs or other destructive behaviors. That, I believe, was the key to my athletic achievements. Even though I sinned, just like everyone else, I always felt checked in my actions. Having lived in a Christian home where the Ten Commandments were our guidelines for right and wrong, I never allowed myself to stray too far from what I'd been taught. Throughout my athletic career, it was important to me to maintain a good reputation, as well as the mutual respect of my fellow athletes.

Now, as a Christian, I realize how important it is to take care of myself physically, not so that I can display to the world any physical prowess, but so that I can honor and glorify God in all areas of my life. And that is what I seek to do now, with whatever time and talents I have to offer. Luke 12:48 says, "To whom much is given, from him much will be required" *(NKJV).* God has blessed me with so much; out of obedience to Him, I am committed to sharing with others out of my own abundance.

☆☆☆

Although I was raised in a Christian home, I didn't truly come to know the Lord until just a few years ago. Having grown up in poverty, I came to believe that if I knew the rules of the game—any game—I could play it better than anybody else. Needless to say, that led to a competitive attitude and a successful athletic career, from All-American status in high school, through my years at UCLA, and on through my 10 years in the NBA playing for the New York Knickerbockers and the Boston Celtics.

It was during my time with the New York Knicks that I first met Rosey Grier, who was then playing football for the New York Giants. We became good friends, and stayed in touch even after I retired from the NBA and moved back to Los Angeles. When Rosey (who, by then, also lived in L.A.), invited me to church, I was more than slightly skeptical. I had long since quit attending church, even though I often thought about my Christian upbringing. In fact, another friend of mine, entertainer Bill Withers, and I had only recently been discussing how we missed the feelings and memories associated with going to church. But, as I told Rosey, I'm like those people from Missouri—you have to show me before I'll believe anything!

Sitting there in church next to Rosey and listening to the pastor speak on the meaning of faith, however, I realized how totally opposite my "show me" attitude was from what the Bible teaches. God's Word says you must first believe, then you will see. Being a strong-willed person with a lot of self-pride, that was hard for me to deal with. But before the service was over, I yielded to the challenge to commit my life to God.

It's a continuing struggle for me, a day-to-day lesson, but I am learning through reading and studying the Word of God, and then I do what the Word says. As I do that, I know that Christ will be exalted, and others will see Jesus in my life.

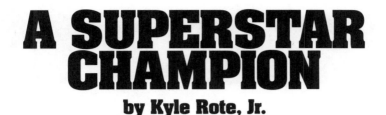

A SUPERSTAR CHAMPION

by Kyle Rote, Jr.

☆ **Kyle Rote, Jr.** ☆

Photo used with permission.

KYLE ROTE, JR. (Soccer)
- Only American-born soccer player to win a major professional soccer league Scoring Championship
- Represented U.S. in international competition 1973-1976
- All-time leading scorer in Dallas Tornado history
- Winner of *Superstars* competition (three times)
- Selected in 1984 as one of "Ten Outstanding Young Men in America"
- Wife: Mary Lynne

"It would be easy for me to adopt a self-sufficient, independent attitude as a result of some of the success I've achieved. But I know that, without Jesus in my life, it would all be hollow and aimless."

IT WAS 1974 WHEN THE CALL CAME FROM THE PROMOTION department of ABC-TV, inviting me to join 47 other professional athletes in a decathlon-type event called the Superstars Competition. I was flattered, but I was also excited. I set out immediately to prepare myself to compete against some of the best known athletes in the country, including Roger Staubach, Lynn Swann, O.J. Simpson, Julius Erving, John Havlicek and Reggie Jackson, among others.

I was excited about the event for several reasons. One, of course, was that the money involved would come in real handy. The other was that it could focus some attention on professional soccer, a sport that is extremely popular in many other countries, but not nearly as well known here in the United States.

Few people gave me much of a chance at winning, but I didn't let that bother me. For weeks, I worked on my tennis game. My wife, Mary Lynne, and I rode bikes everywhere we went. I joined the YMCA and swam daily. In between all that, I practiced my bowling and golf games.

The hard work paid off. In the first round of this two-day, 10-event competition, I won out over such famous athletes as tennis great Rod Laver and baseball stars Reggie Jackson and Jim Palmer. Soon after, during the 1974 Superstar finals, I finished first in the tennis competition, went on to place second in golf, and before the first day was over, I had also won the 100-meter swim and the bowling competition.

I didn't do as well the second day in the baseball hitting or the 880-yard run, but I did manage to finish a strong second in the cycle race. Overall, I had accumulated 44 points, my nearest challenger, 38. I had won the Superstars Competition over the world's most celebrated athletes.

Almost overnight, I went from being a little known soccer star to one of the biggest sports heroes in America. Needless to say, it was an exciting time. The best part of all, however, was having the chance to speak to 60 million people by way of national TV when the event was aired weeks later—to tell them that, although becoming a Superstars champion was very important to me, it was not the center of my life.

That spot was already occupied—and always would be—by my greatest Friend, Jesus Christ.

☆☆☆

I was born in Dallas, Texas, on Christmas Day of 1950. Raised in a Christian home, I attended church primarily to please my parents, but I had little or no interest in the message of the Gospel. I basically thought of my one hour a week in church as "insurance"—if there really was a God and there really was a heaven, maybe attending church regularly would get me in.

Then, the summer before my senior year of high school, I went to a Young Life camp. It was there I realized for the first time that, although I had a lot of athletic talent and ability, I had no purpose in life. I felt as if I had been running in circles, searching for some meaning to it all. That's when I knew that, if I was ever going to do anything worthwhile, I would have to turn my life over to Jesus Christ—and then keep that relationship at the top of my priority list.

And that's exactly what I did. From that point on, I began to notice transformations in my overall attitude. Although I still loved sports, my entire life didn't hinge on the outcome of a particular game. I began to care more about other people. Old habits, such as lying and stealing to impress my friends, began to fade away. I was definitely different.

I believe the reason for that was because I had asked God to change me—and He was faithful in giving me His Spirit to do just that. Also, I had begun to realize that God's love is unconditional. He loves me whether I win or lose, whether I'm successful or unsuccessful. And besides, it puts everything else in perspective when you've read the end of the book and you know that the ultimate victory is already a sure thing.

SUCCESS THAT LASTS

by Barry Sanders

☆ **Barry Sanders** ☆

Photo used with permission.

BARRY SANDERS (Football)

- High School Player of the Year 1986
- College All American Team 1988
- Walter Camp Trophy 1988
- Maxwell Award 1988
- Heisman Trophy 1988
- Pro Bowl 1989
- Rookie of the Year 1989
- Plays with:
    Detroit Lions (current)

"It's a wonderful thing to achieve success in your chosen sport. But the real test comes when things get tough and you have to find out who you are away from that sport."

ONE OF THE FIRST QUESTIONS PEOPLE ASK ME IS, "HOW does it feel to be a Heisman Trophy winner?"

Well, of course, it feels wonderful. Winning the Heisman is a real honor, and I appreciate being chosen to win that honor. There are many fine athletes who have won the award over the years, and I feel privileged to be among them.

Some people, however, have commented that, when they watched me receive the award on television, I didn't seem as excited about winning as they would have expected me to be. Part of that, I suppose, is my "laid-back" attitude. Mostly, though, it's because I realize that all honors and awards—even the Heisman—are temporary. All the glitter and glamour and hype that goes along with being the Heisman Trophy winner will fade someday, and no one will stop me and ask for my autograph anymore. In the long run, there's only one thing that really lasts, one thing that won't fade away, and that's a relationship with Christ.

You see, winning the Heisman Trophy was not the driving force that made me want to play football. I played because it was fun; because I loved the sport. Also, I believe that God gave me the desire and the talent to play the game, and to play it well. I always keep that thought in mind, because as soon as we put something else—sports, people, anything—before our relationship with Christ, things will begin to fall apart in our lives. That's one of the things my parents taught me from the time I was very young. Football is fine. Winning games and awards and honors is great. But it's all temporary. Hang on to what's eternal if you really want to find success in your life.

☆☆☆

I grew up in a large family—eight sisters, two brothers—and we were very close. We were raised in church and our parents taught us how to live by the example they set.

When I was in junior high school, I accepted Christ as my Savior, but I really didn't know Him as Lord until I was in college. That's when I first realized how important it is to draw close to Him when you're faced with trials and temptations, or you will stray away and fall into the ways of the world. I saw it happen to so many people. Morals in college are very loose, and without a strong, consistent relationship with Jesus Christ, it's very hard to resist the temptations around you.

Not only did I see this happen to college kids, I saw it in the newspapers too—stories about athletes sacrificing their careers and ruining their lives with alcohol and drugs. I also had an older brother who was caught up in the things of the world before he became a minister. Seeing all of that was enough to make me hold on to Christ, to be consistent in my prayer and Bible reading, because I knew that was my real source of strength.

That might sound like a funny thing for an athlete to say, because a lot of people think I've got it made since I won the Heisman Trophy. But like I tell them, I haven't always been a Heisman Trophy winner, just like David wasn't always a king. He had to be a shepherd first. But whether you're a shepherd or a king, there's still only one thing that really matters—a relationship with Jesus Christ.

Photo courtesy of The Dallas Cowboys; used with permission.

☆ **Roger Staubach** ☆
See page 205

A LONG SHOT
by Jay Schroeder

☆ **Jay Schroeder** ☆

JAY SCHROEDER
(Football, Baseball)

- Redskin Offensive Player of the Year 1986
- Pro Bowl 1987
- Played with:
  Toronto Bluejays 1979-1983 (baseball)
  Washington Redskins 1984-1987 (football)
  Los Angeles Raiders (football—current)
- Wife: Debbie
- Children: Brian, Christopher

"Success is really just a matter of going out and believing that you can do the job that God wants you to do."

WHEN I FIRST DECIDED TO MAKE THE TRANSITION FROM professional baseball to professional football, a lot of people didn't give me much chance at success. In fact, I was what was known as a "long shot." But I always believed—and I still do—that it's what God wanted me to do.

It was during a Monday night football game against the New York Giants that I first had the opportunity to play in the NFL. I was sitting on the sidelines with my team, the Washington Redskins, when our quarterback, Joe Theismann, was injured. Stepping into his place meant filling some very big shoes—especially because I had never played a single down in the NFL!

But with the assurance that I was in God's will, I went out onto the field and managed to throw a couple of touchdown passes. Not only that, we came from behind and won the game.

Being able to play healthy the entire next season was another blessing. Then, going on to make the Pro-Bowl as a result of the votes of the other players in the league was a very special honor for me.

Choosing to make the move into the NFL may have been a long shot, but now, playing with the Los Angeles Raiders, I can look back on all God has already done and face the future with a confidence and assurance that, whatever opportunities He chooses to bring my way, He will be there to see me through.

☆☆☆

Although I grew up in a Christian home and attended church regularly, I really didn't believe all that I'd been taught and, therefore, hadn't really made a commitment to live for Christ.

When I was about 18 years old, however, I found

myself away from home for the first time. I had followed my dream of being a professional baseball player and made it into the minor leagues. While there, I met some dedicated Christians, got involved in chapel and, in the summer of 1981, accepted the Lord into my life.

Little had I known that, when I followed my dream, it would lead to a lot more than a professional sports career. It would lead to the greatest decision of my entire life—a decision I have never regretted. God has blessed me with some wonderful moments since then—and carried me through the rough ones. But *always* He was there.

SEEING MYSELF THROUGH OTHER PEOPLE'S EYES

by Jackie Slater

☆ **Jackie Slater** ☆

Photo courtesy of the Los Angeles Rams; used with permission.

JACKIE SLATER (Football)

- Offensive Lineman of the Year (three times)
- NFC Pro Bowl Team (five times)
- Plays with:
  Los Angeles Rams (current)
- Wife: Annie Ruth
- Son: Matthew Wilson

"As opposed to making a lot of verbal statements about who I am and the type of life I'm trying to live and the Person I'm trying to follow, I strive to live in such a way that people will realize there's something different about me."

EVEN THOUGH I HAD BECOME A CHRISTIAN WHILE I WAS in college, I still had a terrible temper—and everybody knew it. I was ready to fight anytime, anywhere. Until the Lord let me see myself as others saw me.

I remember it like it was yesterday. There I was, out on the practice field going through one-on-one drive-block drills with the rest of the Los Angeles Rams, when I noticed a problem developing between two of the players. One of them was a long-time veteran, the other a young offensive guard. The young guard was blasting the veteran so hard he was driving him right off the board. After this had happened several times, the veteran got mad and started throwing punches. Before the young guard could fight back, however, it was broken up.

I watched that young guard storm off the field and stand along the sidelines, seething with rage. "That's you, Jackie," the Lord seemed to say to me. "That's just the way you look when you lose your temper."

And I knew it was true, because I knew exactly how that young guard felt. I had stood in his shoes many times, letting my anger control my thoughts and actions.

Then I looked around me at the other players and the coaches. They were staring at the guy, too. That's when I realized what others must have thought of me every time they saw me out of control with anger.

I decided I didn't like what I was seeing. Right then and there, I resolved to seek the Lord's help each and every time I felt myself beginning to lose control to my anger. As long as I have remembered to do that, He has never let me down.

☆☆☆

During my growing-up years in Jackson, Mississippi, I attended church and tried to set a good example for my four younger brothers. But once I went away to college, I gave up all that so I could "do my own thing." Unfortunately, the things I chose to do weren't always the best things for me to be doing. It didn't take long before I had earned a reputation of being a real "bad guy."

In 1974, however, at the end of my sophomore year, I made a commitment to the Lord, but I have to admit, my walk was pretty shaky for the next couple of years—hot one day, cold the next. It wasn't until I was drafted by the Rams and found myself moving from Jackson, Mississippi, to Los Angeles, California, that things began to turn around for me.

In the radically new environment of professional football, in a huge city where I didn't know anyone, I was suddenly dependent on Christ for everything. And the more I turned to Him, the more I saw the results of His faithfulness. He brought many wonderful, strong Christians into my life, people who steered me in the right direction and encouraged me to get involved in a Bible-centered church, to study the Word and pray daily.

Now, in my 14th year with the Rams, I can look back on my life at all the Lord has brought me through, and understand better why things happened the way they did. I can also look forward to whatever God has in store for me in the future. My favorite Bible verse, Romans 8:28, says it this way: "And we know that all things work together for good to those who love God, to those who are the called according to His purpose" (*NKJV*).

A CROWN THAT LASTS FOREVER

by JoJo Starbuck

☆ **JoJo Starbuck** ☆

JOJO STARBUCK
(Figure skating)

- With skating partner Ken Shelley:
    Competed in two Winter Olympic Games
    Twice World Bronze Medalists
    Three-time U.S. Champions
    Starred in Ice Capades
- Competed in The World Professional Championships
- Professional Skater of the Year Award 1983, 1987
- With skating partner and Olympic champion John Curry:
    Performed in "Ice Dancing" (on Broadway and around the world)

"When you think about it, how many things in this constantly changing world can we really count on? Nothing—except God's Word and His Kingdom. And that's the power I want to depend on when I face life's many challenges."

E VER SINCE I CAN REMEMBER, I'VE BEEN EXTREMELY AC-
tive. As a child I was always running, jumping,
dancing, climbing trees or producing plays in my
garage—somehow convincing the neighborhood kids
to act in them, and their parents to come and see us.
There always seemed to be something exciting to con-
quer, from the monkey bars at school to the Hula Hoop
at home.

When my mom—a combination Auntie Mame/
Mama Rose/Lucille Ball and the Unsinkable Molly
Brown—enrolled me in a dance class, I thought I had
arrived! Until I discovered a pair of ice skates under
the Christmas tree, that is. At seven years old, I found
my niche—the perfect outlet for both the actress and
tomboy in me!

When I was eight, I met Ken Shelley, who was to
become my skating partner and good friend for the
next 30 years. Ken's skill and joy for skating matched
mine to a *T*, and together we began to win medals and
trophies each time we competed. In fact, we eventually
went on to win three U.S. Championships, the North
American Championships, bronze medals in two
World Championships, and competed in two Olympic
Games. We turned pro in 1972, skating with the Ice Ca-
pades, doing television specials and touring in various
shows around the world.

Through it all, however, the sacrifices, struggles,
discipline and pressures continued to multiply. It
didn't take me long to learn that a competitive skater
must practice thousands of hours annually, with only
two or three major chances to really prove him or her-
self each year. All the pressure and sacrifice and discipline can rest on one four-minute performance! I

quickly realized I needed more than good training and hard work to get me through those times.

Even today, when I'm pushing myself around the rink, my muscles aching and crying out for me to stop, I remember what it says in 1 Corinthians 9:24, 25:

> *Do you not know that in a race all the runners run, but only one gets the prize? Run in such a way as to get the prize. Everyone who competes in the games goes into strict training. They do it to get a crown that will not last; but we do it to get a crown that will last forever.*

Every athlete knows that the more you exercise your muscles, the more you put them to the test, the more you push them to the limit, the stronger and more capable and dependable those muscles become. It may hurt during the process, but the feeling of achievement, strength and victory that comes later is worth it all. And how much greater is that feeling when it involves a crown that will last forever!

☆☆☆

My red-haired Irish mom took me to church every Sunday morning. She taught me the value of prayer and told me about our loving God. I went to classes faithfully and learned all my lessons. Never having known my earthly father who died when I was young, I loved the idea of being able to talk to my Father in heaven. I especially liked the idea that He loved me enough to help and bless me; that's very exciting to a fatherless kid!

But even with all that, I knew there had to be more. The whole "church experience" seemed so far away and impersonal. I wanted to raise my hand during the sermon to ask questions or make comments—anything to get closer to God in an intimate and tangible way. Then, one day in 1969 in a college speech class, it all began to come together.

Our teacher had asked us to stand and introduce ourselves. When a pretty blonde girl stood up and gave her Christian testimony, I was in awe. I knew she had what I'd been searching for all along—a dynamic, personal relationship with God, one that made a real difference in her everyday life—and I wanted it, too. But I was afraid to approach her about it, because every time I tried, I felt like I was going to cry. (Crying in a college hallway is definitely not cool!)

Finally, I worked up the nerve to walk up to her and blurt out, "I want to know more about that born again stuff, but I'm in a hurry to get to the ice rink right now." She just smiled and handed me a booklet on the four spiritual laws. I grabbed it and ran for the parking lot.

As I raced down the freeway, I somehow managed to read through the booklet. (In case you're wondering how I did that, just remember that I'm the same girl who learned to put on panty hose and mascara while burning up the road between point A and point B!)

Anyway, when I saw the diagram showing man at the bottom and God at the top, separated by sin but with Jesus in the middle bridging the gap, I suddenly understood: Jesus is the way to get to know and get close to God—the only way! I immediately said the prayer in the booklet—and my life has never been the same since.

Now, that's not to say that everything's been perfect from that day on. A failed marriage some years ago brought me considerable pain, and moving to

New York City to start a business has been a tough challenge. There have been many times I felt scared, overwhelmed, depressed and drained. But God is always there to carry me through. He is my partner and counselor—even though I don't always listen or understand. And I know now that the things that have happened in my life are all part of His wonderful plan to bring me to a place where I have an opportunity to tell others about His great love.

PUTTING IT ALL IN PERSPECTIVE

by Roger Staubach

☆ **Roger Staubach** ☆

Photo used with permission.

ROGER STAUBACH (Football)

- Heisman Trophy 1963
- NFL Players MVP 1971
- Texas Pro Athlete of the Year 1975
- Vince Lombardi Sportsman of the Year 1975
- NFC Pro Bowl Selection 1972, 1977, 1978, 1979, 1980
- NFL Leading Passer 1978-1980
- NFC Offensive Player of the Year 1978
- Pro Football Hall of Fame 1985
- Played with:
  Dallas Cowboys
- Wife: Marianne
- Children: Jennifer, Michelle, Stephanie, Jeff, Amy

"You can't make faith a part of your portfolio. It must be encompassed in every area of your life."

As an athlete I had a lot of confidence in my abilities and what I could accomplish. This confidence came from two primary sources: First, I knew I had prepared myself for the moment through a lot of hard work (for which there is no substitute!); second, I was able to keep the moment—no matter how crucial—in right perspective. I knew the outcome of that particular moment wasn't the end of the world; there would always be another game, another big moment.

I have always believed—and I still do—that every athlete must perform at the highest level possible in all situations. I was able to do that because I knew the situation was temporary. Our permanence is our faith in Jesus Christ. There is a consistency and balance that comes from knowing and believing that fact.

Whether I was playing in the last seconds of a game against the Minnesota Vikings, a playoff game against the San Francisco 49ers, or in my last regular season game against the Washington Redskins, I was able to persevere in each of those tough moments because of my hard work and because of my faith.

It was that faith that enabled me to handle the major victories with humility, and maintain a proper perspective during the losses.

☆☆☆

There were a lot of influences in my early years—family, school, church—that affected all issues of my life, including my faith. But I believe that everyone has to come to a point of making a permanent decision about a relationship with Jesus Christ. For me, that time came when I was in high school.

Studying the lives of the Apostles helped bring me to that point. The Apostles doubted, denied, even betrayed Jesus Christ—until they saw Him as the Risen Lord. Even then, Thomas had to put his hand into His side before he could be sure that He was indeed the One who had died for our sins and come back for our salvation.

We aren't able to stand before the Risen Lord and see or touch Him as the Apostles did, but that's where faith comes in. Up until the time in high school when I made a personal decision about Jesus Christ, I had to rely on reasoning, the Scriptures, and the influence and teachings of others. Faith, however, filled the void those other elements could not, the same void the Apostles had until they saw and touched Him.

We all live and work within certain boundaries, and sometimes we get backed up against what I consider some of the most important boundaries of all, boundaries that challenge our moral standards. But Jesus is our example; faith in Him will keep us within the right boundaries. It will also give us a proper balance in everything we do in life.

FINDING THE TRUE SOURCE OF STRENGTH

by John Washington

☆ **John Washington** ☆

JOHN WASHINGTON (Football)
- Second Team All-Big Eight 1983-1985
- Honorable Mention, All-American Team Captain 1985
- Defensive End with New York Giants (current)
- Wife: Terri
- Children: Charmaine, John, Jr.

"If I could say just one thing to young people today, it would be to choose your friends carefully. If you listen to the wrong advice and follow the wrong people, you're going to end up on the wrong road. But if you listen to Jesus Christ and follow Him, He will steer you in the right direction."

I KNOW IT MUST BE DISCOURAGING TO A LOT OF PEOPLE, young people especially, to see so many of their sports idols falling. But being out there in the middle of it all, I am excited to see how many athletes are *not* falling. In fact, they're standing stronger than ever, because more and more of them are coming to a point of discovering the true Source of their strength—Jesus Christ.

Many of the professional teams—baseball, football, basketball—now have regular chapel services. And it's encouraging to see how well attended they are, not just by players, but by coaches, too. In fact, I never set foot on the field without calling the team together for a pre-game prayer. Between our prayers, our fellowship and our chapel services, we have established a true family atmosphere.

Now, not just on the football field, but everywhere I go, I remember that my actions can have a deep effect on those who are watching me—my own two children, as well as thousands of other children who just happen to be football fans looking for a hero to imitate.

☆☆☆

As a young child, I thought I was a Christian. But it wasn't until the end of my sophomore year of high school that I truly understood what being a Christian really meant.

I was 16 years old. Throughout my 16 years of life, my grandfather had been a real role model for me. I loved him very much, and had depended on him as a source of strength.

And then he died. Suddenly, I found myself without that dependable source of strength I had relied on for years. I was very hurt, and felt very much alone.

Out of that loss and hurt, I turned to Jesus Christ. For the first time, I found out what true strength was. In my personal life and in my football career, I have looked to Him as my source of strength ever since.

FOLLOWING THE LEADER

by Reggie White

☆ **Reggie White** ☆

REGGIE WHITE (Football)
- Runner-up, Vince Lombardi Award 1983
- Defensive Rookie of the Year, USFL 1984, 1985
- Man of the Year, USFL 1985
- Pro Bowl MVP 1987
- Pro Bowl participant 1986-1988
- NFL Alumni Defensive Player of the Year 1987-1988
- Played with:
  Memphis Showboat (USFL) 1984-1985
  Philadelphia Eagles (current)
- Wife: Sara
- Children: Jeremy, Jecolia

"So many young people look up to us as athletes. It's important that we make a positive difference in their lives to help counteract the negative images they see portrayed in the media. Kids need role models who exemplify honesty and commitment."

ONE OF THE ROUGHEST PERIODS I EVER EXPERIENCED IN my career was during my junior year in college. I suffered so many injuries—two sprained ankles, a chipped bone in my elbow, a pinched nerve in my neck. On top of all that, I was criticized by the media. They hinted that my injuries were due to the fact that I wasn't tough enough on the football field because I was a Christian.

Of course, that wasn't true. The real reason I continued getting hurt was because I wasn't in as good a physical condition as I should have been. And that was because I had settled for being a follower instead of a leader.

Time after time, I would tell myself I needed to go to the gym and work out. My friends and teammates, however, would talk me into skipping my workout and doing something else with them instead. Although I enjoyed being with my friends, my physical condition was slipping and my injuries were increasing.

That's when I decided I needed to change. I asked God to give me the strength to become a leader. As I committed myself to do the things I needed to do, my friends began to follow me. When I turned down their invitations and went on to the gym to work out, they came along and worked out, too. That's when I knew that God had really turned things around for me.

The next year was the best season of my college career. Funny thing, though. The media, who had previously criticized me for not being tough enough because I was a Christian, now began to criticize me for being too tough. But I didn't really care, because I knew that God had really turned my situation around by helping me become the leader He had called me to be.

☆☆☆

I spent a lot of time in church when I was a kid, and I grew up hearing about the need to be "saved." So, every time I sinned, I answered the altar call to get saved again!

But one night, when I was 13, I was attending a Bible study when someone asked me if I was saved. I told them I sure was, that I'd been saved lots of times. That was the first time anyone ever took the time to explain to me what salvation really was—and that once was enough! I've always been glad that I came to know the Lord at such a young age, but it wasn't until I was grown and married that God really challenged me to become all that I could be for Him.

You see, athletes are under a lot of pressure, pressure that can affect all areas of their lives. One of these areas is marriage. I was once at a point where my marriage was seriously threatened. I wanted to leave my wife. But God showed me that I was taking the easy way out. He challenged me to stay and to become the husband that my wife needed me to be, the father that my children needed me to be.

Because I answered that challenge, our marriage is now a solid one. I realize, too, that as important as my career is to me, ministering to my home and family must always come first.

COMMITTING MY WAY

by Wendy White

☆ **Wendy White** ☆

WENDY WHITE (Tennis)
- All-American (high school and college)
- Alford Scholarship Award 1979
- *Tennis Magazine* Player of the Year 1980
- Broderick Award 1980
- AIAW finalist 1979
- AIAW Champion 1980

"One of the most exciting things that ever happened to me was when I realized that having Jesus in my life changed my 'have-to's' to 'want-to's.'"

I T was June 1980, my last collegiate-level tournament before turning pro. I was nervous but excited
as I prayed and searched the Scriptures that morning,
confident of God's assurance that now was the time to
make the switch from college-level competition to the
professional ranks. I had made it all the way to the national finals the previous year, only to be eliminated at
the end. This year, however, I felt sure of a win.

"Delight yourself also in the Lord," I read in Psalm
37:4,5, "And He shall give you the desires of your
heart. Commit your way to the Lord, Trust also in
Him, and He shall bring it to pass" (NKJV). Shortly after
coming across that Scripture, my mother came into my
room and confirmed God's Word when she explained
that the Lord had laid those very same verses on her
heart to share with me. My faith soared! I was ready.

But that afternoon, when I got out on the court in
front of the TV cameras and commentators and specta-
tors, I was tense, tentative—and my style showed it. I
lost the first set, and was well on my way to losing the
second when I heard one of the commentators say,
"The games seem to be slipping away from Wendy."

Suddenly I realized that I had forgotten the most
important part of that Scripture in Psalm 37, the part
that says, "*Commit* your way to the Lord, *Trust* also in
Him, and *He* shall bring it to pass." I had committed
my way to the Lord up until that match, but then had
begun relying on my own abilities, rather than His. As
I prayed and released myself, as well as the outcome of
the tournament, to God, I felt myself relax. Not only
did I go on to win that game and match, I won the
whole thing—the Nationals!

The lesson I learned that day, however, was not a
one-time thing. As I have gone on in my walk with the

Lord, as well as in my ten-year pro-tennis career, I have had to remind myself of that lesson every single day. And each day I recommit my way to Him, trusting in Him to accomplish what only He can do. As another verse proclaims, "The Lord will accomplish what concerns me" (Ps. 138:8, NASB).

☆☆☆

I had a wonderful upbringing, an almost ideal childhood. I was raised in a warm, supportive family. I attended church and participated in the youth group. We had a Bible in our house and said grace before meals. But in all those years of growing up, I never heard anyone talk about God as if they truly knew Him.

Not until I was in high school, that is. I was attending a private school. My New Testament class teacher was a dedicated Christian. He encouraged us to memorize Scripture for extra credit, talked about his experiences as a Christian, and set an example for his students to follow. It was his explanation of Ephesians 2:8,9—"For it is by grace you have been saved, through faith—and this not from yourselves, it is the gift of God—not by works, so that no one can boast"—that first opened my eyes to the fact that salvation was a gift, not something I could ever possibly earn for myself.

And then I went away to college. My roommate was a Christian, as well as a fellow tennis player. The two of us began to search for a church to attend. At one of those churches, two guys invited us to a Bible study. Sitting in that Bible study as about 20 people read the Bible, studied the Scriptures and talked about Jesus Christ as if He were their very best friend, I just listened, taking it all in. At the end of the study, the leader asked if there was anyone who wanted to make a commitment (or a recommitment) to Jesus Christ. Then he asked if there was anyone who wasn't *absolutely sure* of salvation. That's when I knew he was talking to me. Although everything in my life seemed to be going great, deep down I wasn't sure whether or not I really had a relationship with Jesus. So I made the simplest—but also the most profound—decision of my life. I responded to the invitation, and suddenly I knew—beyond a shadow of a doubt—that Christ had come into my life.

I had finally found what I'd been searching for all my life. From that point on I never again doubted that I was a Christian, because I had come to understand what being a Christian really means—and that is, to have Jesus Christ living within me.

MY ULTIMATE "PEAK" EXPERIENCE

by John Wooden

☆ **John Wooden** ☆

JOHN WOODEN (Basketball)

- All-American Purdue University 1930-1932
- College Basketball Player of the Year 1932
- NBA Hall of Fame (as a player) 1960
- NBA Hall of Fame (as a coach) 1972
- College "Coach of the Year" (six times)
- Friars Club "Coach of the Century" 1971
- *Sports Illustrated* "Sportsman of the Year" 1973
- California "Sports Father of the Year" 1975
- Wife: Nellie (deceased)
- Children: Nancy Anne, James Hugh

"Faith is not just waiting, hoping, and wanting things to happen. Rather it is working hard to make things happen and realizing that there are no failures—just disappointments—when you have done your best."

As I TURNED AWAY FROM THE POST-GAME PRESS CONFER-
ence and headed down that long corridor in
Kansas City toward the dressing room, my feet and
spirits dragged. For while I looked forward to congrat-
ulating the team on their victory, my thoughts were
also on Fred Slaughter. What was he feeling at this moment?

Throughout the entire season, Fred had started
every game. He had a brilliant year. Fred was a totally
unselfish player with great team devotion and was fre-
quently asked to do things for which a player receives
little public attention. Even though he was short for a
college center, barely 6 feet 5 inches tall, Fred was the
blocker, screener, and rebounder—things seldom seen
and appreciated by the crowd. But in this final game
for the championship with Duke he had gotten off to a
bad start. As the game moved along, it got worse instead of better. Finally, a change had to be made, so I
pulled Fred and put in Doug McIntosh. And Doug did
such a fine job that I left him in until the game was
ours.

Pushing open the dressing room door, I ran right
into Fred. He had evidently been waiting for me.
"Coach," he said, "before someone gets the wrong im-
pression, I want you to know that I understand. You
had to leave Doug in there because he played so well,
and I didn't. I wanted to play in the worst way, but I
do understand, and if anyone says I was upset, it's not
true. Disappointed, yes, but upset, no. And I was very
happy for Doug."

You know, there are a lot of peaks and valleys in
every coach's life. But this was *the* peak—the ultimate.
We had won our first, and my first, NCAA title by

whipping Duke 98 to 83 and closed out the 1964 season with a perfect 30 and 0 record. But my concern for Fred had damaged all of that until this moment. Now I felt really great!

☆☆☆

My life has been wrapped around the family structure and the church from my earliest memory. My personal family life is merely an extension of a life-style formed in my boyhood with my mother, father, and brothers.

A truly gentle man, Dad read the Bible daily; he wanted us to read it, and we did. That is probably why I keep a copy on my desk today. It is not a decoration, but is well marked and read. The fact that I never heard Dad swear surely accounts for the fact that even today when I get mad, the strongest thing I can say is "goodness gracious sakes alive."

My dad did love his fellowman sincerely. He was honest to the nth degree and had a great trust and faith in the Lord. And he taught us many lessons in integrity and honesty which we never forgot.

The most important thing I ever learned in all my years, however, is that basketball is not the ultimate. It is of small importance in comparison to the total life we live. There is only one kind of a life that truly wins, and that is the one that places faith in the hands of the Savior. Until that is done, we are on an aimless course that runs in circles and goes nowhere. Material possessions, winning scores, and great reputations are meaningless in the eyes of the Lord, because He knows what we really are and that is all that matters.

*Adapted from *They Call Me Coach* by John Wooden (Waco, Texas: Word, Inc., 1972). Used by permission.